TOTAL SOCCER COACHING
Combining Physical, Technical and Tactical Training

Riccardo Capanna - Marco Oneto - Gianni Ferrera

D1333931

Learning Resources
Centre

**Library of Congress
Cataloging - in - Publication Data**

by R. Capanna - M. Oneto - G. Ferrera
    TOTAL SOCCER COACHING

ISBN No. 1-59164-057-1
Lib. of Congress Catalog No. 2003108194
© 2003

Editing
Bryan R. Beaver

Printed by
DATA REPRODUCTIONS
Auburn, Michigan

Reedswain Publishing
612 Pughtown Road
Spring City, PA 19475
800.331.5191
www.reedswain.com
info@reedswain.com

CONTENTS

PREFACE

The single message this book desires to deliver to coaches is: "It is possible to learn to improve one's own coaching methods". It is especially dedicated to all those coaches who are involved in Soccer Schools, in the Youth Sector and in the Amateur divisions; however, professional team coaches will also find interesting cues.

It is divided into four chapters: chapter one explains the concepts that will enable the reader to better understand our point of view on the problems related to coaching technical skills.

To us, coaching is synonymous with "teaching", that "art" that makes possible the transfer of knowledge from one individual to another.

Learning to teach is then the main objective of a coach. Learning to teach can be accomplished only through a long, complex and never ending path, continuously searching for improvements.

Improving their own ability to teach is the motivation that should guide all the coaches who are constantly concerned about improving their players' level of learning.

In Chapter two, we introduce our practical proposal. It is based on common physiological, neuro-physiological and psycho-cognitive principles, therefore the ideas explained are not new but are a useful reminder of fundamental concepts.

We firmly believe that there should be a consistency between the theoretical concepts that guide us and the practical applications that we suggest, with the main objective of distancing ourselves from preconceptions that in the past have generated unworkable approaches to teaching and learning methods.

In the same way, we reject preconceptions about the player's ability or inability to learn and concepts that have no cultural basis.

The third chapter contains some exercises, explained with diagrams and text that can be useful to help the technical development of young soccer players.

In the fourth chapter, there are some in-depth analyses related to subjects that are dealt with in the first two chapters, in which the sequence of the sections follows the logical succession of the contents. In this way, the reader can better understand the ideas without having to read the in-depth analyses in detail.

We would like to thank all our friends, coaches and trainers, who have been helpful by reviewing, analyzing and making suggestions for the presentation of the subject matter of this book.

Special thanks to Ugo Giovanni Foscolo and Enrico Calvi, who have helped us in the revision of this book, thus helping us to present an improved final product.

The Authors

INTRODUCTION

Ten years ago, when we published "Non solo muscoli - I processi cognitive nello sport" , our objective was to demonstrate to both trainers and coaches the necessity of planning coaching activities with the understanding that each individual is an **inseparable biological, psychical and social unit**, no matter the activity he is required to perform.

By observing the way that coaches continued to coach, we had the impression that we had not managed to make them understand the necessity of considering coaching as a **total** process, which involves both the athletic-physical sphere and the coordination sphere (currently, technical tactical coaching is separate from conditioning). So, we wrote "I muscoli al servizio di Sua Maestà il Cervello" , in which we suggested exercises in which the objectives of the two spheres overlapped and which we called "Special Physical Conditioning" (SPC).

Finally, in the spring of the year 2000, we wrote "Riflessioni e proposte per il gioco del calcio" , in which we suggested a new kind of activity which we called "match exercise".

The importance that we attach to SPC and to match exercise is a result of our belief that together they are a model of performance in which the individual is involved as a bio-psycho-social unit. Thus, the model meets the needs related to physical adaptation, coordination and tactical cooperation.

In this book, the main subject is once again: "How do we develop the player's conditional abilities and technical-tactical abilities at the same time?".

The classic theory of coaching, mostly structured to solve the problems of individual sports, is characterized by a method almost totally focused on the development of the player's physical abilities.

In the same way, the studies on skills coaching have developed following the theory of motor learning, suggesting coaching sequences structured according to principles of common sense (for example, from easy to difficult; from slow to fast movement).

Therefore, the present trend continues to be to separately carry out conditioning training from technical-tactical coaching. This entails the alternating presence of the coach and of the physical trainer, according to a structured plan. Using a simile, we could say that it is as though the coach and the physical trainer have to fill two different "tanks", and the athlete is the mixer in which the different elements are combined to give the result of so much effort: **sports fitness.**

Although we consider this approach to be outdated, many coaches and trainers consider this approach to be correct and give the following reasons.

The first is that, according to them, using the ball it is not possible to reach either a **high intensity** of the coaching work load or substantial increase in the **amount** of work as far as the energy released by the biomechanical mechanisms is concerned. In other words, the technical aspect of the movement is considered a factor that limits physical conditioning. This idea is influenced by the works of Matwejew , in which the formal aspect of the movement is not considered: as a result, one parameter of the coaching workload such as the **quality** of the movement is underestimated.

The second of these reasons is related to the theory of the development of **movement**, which stems from what we believe are outdated notions. According to this theory, fatigue is a factor that limits the ability to make a correct movement, and, therefore, they believe it can be inferred that skills can be learned better in a situation in which the player is not tired.

We do not agree with these ideas; we believe that the planning of the coaching of a soccer team should include a considerable amount of time in which the players play with the ball, and believe that this is the most useful way of coaching.

Let us explain why

All the experts on studies of man recognize that an individual is **a biological, psychological and social unit**.

The biological component and the player's coordination determine an athlete's ability to give a technical performance. This ability, through the social aspect of the performance, enables him to carry out an individual or a team performance.

Therefore, we can state that sports performance is produced by an individual personality that acts in a team setting.

In a team process, one individual member is not sufficient to guarantee the perfect functioning of the whole system.

This means that it is not useful to persist in wanting to improve every part of "system-Man" by addressing every aspect "separately" (skills, tactics, aerobic mechanism, anaerobic mechanism, lactacid or alactacid anaerobic mechanism, various types of expression of strength, etc.) and to persist in considering the results of the tests as the measure of a presumed and achieved sports fitness.

Man is a complex system, made up of all the **specific relationships of his simple parts**, which determine **the development of new characteristics**, which cannot be traced back to the characteristics of their single components.

Therefore, the coaching exercises are particularly useful if they enable the individual parts of "system-Man" to be in a functional relationship to one another, since the level of performance is not determined by the sum of the functioning of the parts.

In order to improve the physical performance of the athlete while he is making, with or without the ball, **the typical movements** of soccer, it is necessary to refer to a new method based on what we could call the theory of **motor action**.

As we have already said, the performance of a player during a match is not simply the "sum" of the individual abilities he has acquired. On the contrary, it is the result of their integration. Therefore, all the components of the performance must be coached at the same time, and the exercises must be "oriented" toward the needs of the match.

At this point it is necessary to deal with the **size** of the coaching workload and how this factor influences the targeted adaptation.

If we reason only in terms of **amount** of the coaching workload, then we are off course. In our previous book , we showed that an exercise can be considered "good" not on the basis of a **pre-established** duration of a repetition or of a sequence of repetitions (quantity), but according to the athlete's ability to keep constant - in time - the level of the **quality** (the way in which he performs) and of the **intensity** (the space-time ratio) of the movement which is carried out in the repetitions.

The quality of the specific movement is checked during each relatively short repetition: as the work is **intermittent**, it is easy to check if the motor performance of the athletes remains constant enough or if there are significant drops in the performance that suggest the exercise be interrupted.

We think it is time for us to make our experience, gained by studying the athletes' learning problems and Cognitive Sciences, available to the needs of coaches.

Before starting, however, we would like coaches to reflect on the following questions:

Do you think that we should keep on considering the soccer player "different" from all other athletes, and that for this reason we should coach him as if he were made up of separate (physical, technical and tactical) compartments?

Or do you think that there might be the possibility of conceiving a new theory and method of **motor action***, with the objective of satisfying the concept of man in his oneness?*

CHAPTER ONE

What does cognitive science state?

The process of learning and improving technical skills can be divided into three parts (see "In-depth analysis 1").

First phase
In the first phase, the basic movements, even combined, are developed in a favorable and simplified learning situation. The exercises must be frequently repeated and, in the same session, must be separated from one another by complete recovery. The repetitions are limited in number to those corresponding to the moment when the athlete's mistakes in motor performance occur.

Second phase
The various technical exercises are repeated, in different situations. In this phase, the coach pre-establishes in every exercise the variations that the player will have to practice. The player is more involved than in the previous phase, as he is in a context of medium difficulty.

Third phase
There is a further development and improvement of the movements that the player will have to make as the context varies.
It is a learning condition which is made difficult on purpose. The moves and the situations are not pre-established: the athlete must prove that he is in a position to give adequate responses to the incidental situations.

What has changed
Experts agree that it is only for the first phase of the development of new learning that teaching can be connected with the classic rules established by cognitive theory (see "In-depth analysis 2).
The coach must help the young player to focus on only a few elements. In order to do this, the environment of play and the exercise must facilitate his task.
As for the last two phases of learning, the objective of which is to improve the acquired movements, Cognitive Sciences have made great progress relative to "methods".
One conclusion that has been reached is that the relationship between

technical development and physical-tactical development must somehow change, as a positive effect on motor coordination has been observed when there is an increase in body temperature caused by a conditional load.

Also, it has been noticed that medium and high intensity conditional loads can have better effects on the coaching of technical skills than maximum intensity conditional loads.

This means that conditioning training and coaching of technical skills can be successfully combined provided that (1) the muscles involved in both activities are not required to carry out extreme anaerobic-alactacid exercises (strength-based activities with high overloads), and (2) the muscles do not reach their maximum level of metabolic acidity (lactacid ability exercises).

Therefore, in learning technical skills, the **quality** of the movement and the **intensity** with which it is carried out are both important. It is only after the correct combination of quality and intensity of the exercises, thereby stimulating the proper muscles and setting the proper space/time parameters of the movement, that the **quantity** and the **persistence** of the stimulation become important. It is only by repeating the exercise over and over in time that adaptation to the environment is achieved.

The coach must overcome the fear that conditioning training, producing a certain fatigue in the athlete's body, has a negative effect on coordination. Of course, fatigue can generate a certain deterioration in the performance of a movement; however, it is a fundamental stimulation in a complex activity like soccer, in which there is the need for the player to make decisions about his movements as he progresses through stages of fatigue. In addition, under certain conditions it is acceptable to apply stronger stimulation than the ones the athlete usually experiences during a match. This permits the player to become accustomed to playing in critical conditions, and therefore might be useful in certain moments of a real match.

How does the environment influence the abilities?

When he plays, the soccer player expresses a coordinated and specific motor activity which is characteristic of his sport.

His successful technical-tactical performance in a match depends on how well he has learned from the stimulation received from the coaching "environment" established by the coach. On the other hand, the match creates **psychological pressure** which can negatively influence the player. This is why the coaching session needs to be organized in such a way as to stimulate both the player's technical-tactical development as well as his ability to deal with ever more complex emotional situations.

Let us consider now when it is that the player is most likely to have difficulty because of psychological pressure brought about by his need "to be successful".

Pressure due to the need to "be precise"

When a player tries to be precise in his **technical** performance, the control of the movement is kinesthetic and conscious, therefore not, by itself, very profitable.

On the other hand, when a player tries to be precise in the **result** and relies on his own style, the control of his movement is profitable as it is focused on the effect of his action, and is called "visual-perceptive-motor".

As these are two different neuro-physiological mechanisms, both of them need to be addressed in coaching in order to improve the player's technical performance, keeping in mind that it is the latter mechanism that a player will use in a match and therefore must learn to use in a natural way.

Time pressure

This occurs when a player must carry out a motor task which involves a strong relationship between **speed of movement and technical precision**.

- the **speed of movement** is used to respond to an environmental stimulation and depends on the ability to properly activate visual-perceptive-motor processes. For example, the player reads the situation of play in anticipation and gets to the ball before his opponent.
- the **technical precision** with which a motor action is carried out depends on the player's coordination ability. For example, the player anticipates his opponent with a technically correct and profitable movement.

The problems related to "precision" can also be observed when, for example, the player is asked to play using only one touch. The possible mistakes, especially in the younger players, are mostly due to not having developed, or sufficiently practiced, the specific perceptive processes of that kind of exercise. Therefore, the result is greatly influenced by the necessity to make a movement without having the time to analyze the information from the surrounding environment.

Pressure due to having to make a complex movement

Difficulty in expressing oneself with precision increases when:

-        There are numerous options for movement.
         In sports like soccer, the player has more options to choose from, and therefore more possibilities of making mistakes than athletes with a more limited motor choice (for example, in cycling, track, swimming).

-        The movements must be made while the player is in a condition of uncertain balance.
         These are the actions taken while running, jumping, standing on one foot, being marked by the opponent or on a slippery ground, etc.

-        The player must make multiple movements at the same time.
         For example, when a player has to defend himself from the opponent while at the same time keeping possession of the ball: here, it is more difficult to be precise than where movements are sequential.

-        Many body parts are involved in the player's movement.
         The movements in soccer typically involve the whole body, therefore increasing considerably the difficulty in being precise.

Pressure due to tactical requirements (presence of teammates and opponents)

The complexity of the situation also affects the effectiveness of the technical movement.

Fewer mistakes are made in a tactical context which is "familiar" than are made in a tactical context determined by the opponents, since in the latter the players need to adapt to the changes of play with different time and space organization.

Pressure due to physical-athletic requirements imposed by the match

The coordination and the precision of the movement also depend on both the duration of the performance and on the consequent ability to maintain endurance, as well as on the capacity of strength necessary to make the movement.

This is the only moment when there is a definite correlation between mistakes and the degree of proper physical-athletic conditioning.

Pressure due to "having to prove"

In a match, the pressure from the importance of the score, the presence of the spectators, the prize to be won, the necessity not to make mistakes, etc., may undermine the players' technical skills.

The figure of the coach

The way in which the coach conveys his experience to the players is critical:

- He must always be positive and encouraging, even if he often knows in advance that the result of the player's action will not be positive.

  For example:

  • Try again, you'll see you can do better.

  • Anyone can make a mistake, try to follow what I tell you and you'll see that you'll do better.

- He must ask a lot of questions.

  For example:

  • What are you going to do now?

  • Where did you make a mistake, in your opinion?

  • If you kicked the ball too high, how can you make up for it?

  • Why haven't you passed the ball to George?

- He must not judge mistakes negatively. The mistake must be pointed out, but not underlined with expressions like the following:

  • That was a horrible mistake.

  • Only you could have made such a poor decision.

- Especially at the beginning, he must not point out only those mistakes that are due to incorrect position of the body, but also those related to **timing** (see In-depth analysis n.3).

- With young players, he must consider that some technical mistakes are due to physical-athletic deficiencies, so his demands must be appropriate.

- He must consider that some of the mistakes that he points out are not perceived as mistakes by the players. Therefore, it is useless to suggest corrections that will not be applied. This happens more frequently during the technical coaching phase, when the player must perceive information about himself and his movement.
  For example:
  - Try not to keep your foot too wide out.
  - Your supporting foot during the shot was not properly oriented.
  - You did not raise your arms during the header.

- He must first of all correct the mistake relative to the task, rather than the mistake relative to the wrong movement.
  For example:
  - You shot too high.
  - Your pass was not precise.

- He must be aware that the player is more likely to automatically make those movements that he recognizes as useful to accomplish the optimum objective.

The importance of having a method

The coaching method must help a player to learn, without changing what he has already learned.
The correction of each mistake is important, but it is necessary only when, at the root of the technical form of the movement, there is an incorrect structure that prevents any further improvement of learning the technical skill.
During a **technical exercise**, the coach's advice and corrections must be communicated differently, depending on the particular moment:
- when the player gathers information from the play environment;
- when he processes the information;
- when he passes on to practical application.

If the player is in the phase in which he **gathers information**, the coach's words must optimize the player's perception of the environment and his advice must be individualized.
- He must require the players to consider where and what to look at.
  For example:
  - Before passing the ball, look at where your teammate is (is he

staying put, is he coming toward you, is he getting away from you?).

- Wait for your teammate's eye contact before passing him the ball.
- Try to understand where your teammate would like you to pass him the ball.
- Before shooting, look at the goalkeeper.

- When cooperation with teammates is involved, he can advise the player to consider what changes are occurring around him before starting an action.
  For example:
  - Keep the ball until your teammate comes toward you.
  - Wait for your teammate to get out of the "screened" zone.

If the player is in the phase of **processing**, the coach's words must provide a cognitive and emotional support.
For example:
The coach can ask the player to concentrate on his task and to think about the fact that what he is doing is important for the whole team, etc.

If the player is in the phase of **application**, the coach's advice must aim at improving the quality of coordination.
For example:
- Control the pass.
- Defend the ball better.
- Kick the ball in such a way as to make it pass over the opponents.

As for the coaching of tactics, we recommend the following:
- especially in a youth team, the coach should draw any new tactic on a blackboard before coaching it. This helps the players to understand it better, as the new tactic is seen from above.
  In fact, if the same explanation is given on the field, the perspective might not be clear to the players relative to the distances.

- The coach must give all the tactical information which is necessary to perform the exercise correctly, but avoid giving too much information all at once. He must give the player the opportunity to reach on his own the solution to a problem. He can do this selectively, by giving encouragement and by giving subsequent corrections, which the player can apply the next time he is asked to solve a problem.

In fact, in an exercise that aims at coaching **tactical cooperation**, the coach can give advice before or during the activity.

As for the information given **before the beginning of the exercise**, one important consideration is that in some situations too much information could create inhibition in the players. The coach's words should help the player to:

- Reinforce his self-esteem.

  For example:

  - I am sure that, if you look around more carefully, you can make it.
  - If you concentrate, you are more likely to make a successful pass to your supporting teammate.

- Guide his attention.

  For example:

  - Pay attention to the speed of your pass, or your teammate might not be able to get the ball.
  - Before making the pass, make sure that your defender cannot intercept the ball.

- Help him anticipate the development of the play.

  For example:

  - If you go too close to the end-line, you will run out of space to make the cross.
  - If you are turned toward your own goal, an opponent could pressure you and you wouldn't be able to kick the ball forward.

- Increase his level of awareness.

  For example:

  - If an opponent applies pressure on you from the right, what should you do to start an attack?
  - If one of your teammates overlaps, what are your options?

-   Stimulate his memory.
    For example:
    -   Do you remember what George did before?
    -   Do you remember what happened after Charles crossed the ball?
    -   Do you remember why you made a mistake?

-   Activate those actions which enable him to take time away from the opponent.
    For example:
    -   When the opponent dribbles the ball back, move forward and close off his space of action.
    -   Get closer to the opponent you have to tackle while the ball is still moving; do not wait to mark him after he has received the ball.
    -   If your direct opponent has difficulty in controlling the ball, tackle him.

As for the information given **during the performance of an exercise**, the coach must first of all make sure it does not disturb the players' concentration.
The coach's words must support the player's motivation, for example:
-   Don't worry, keep on defending.
-   Next time pay more attention to your teammates' movement.
-   Try not to let yourself be beaten.
-   Play closer to the side, so that you have more chances to show what you can do.

Finally, the technical-tactical information given **during the match** and conveyed by words or gestures must be similar in form to the information given during the coaching session. This will allow immediate understanding and an easier solution of the problems noticed by the coach.

CHAPTER TWO

Theoretical bases

Technical skills are reflected in specific and targeted movements that a player makes to obtain maximum performance from a motor action.

It is also possible to obtain very good results (shots, passes, control of the ball, dribbling the ball, etc.) through "adapted and personalized technical skills". Taken altogether, these are commonly referred to as **"style of play"** and are characteristic of every individual player.

Therefore, a coach must learn to observe not so much **how** a player makes a certain movement, as whether the player manages to give concrete form to his **intention** (see In-depth analysis n.4).

With younger players, it is important to remember that, in addition to style, they need to develop a **"tactical conduct"** of their own (see In-depth analysis n.5).

"Individual tactical conduct", which is the way in which a player faces the opponent while trying to derive benefit for himself or for the team, is expressed by the player's ability to make individual or team **feints**.

So-called **"group tactics"** refers to the situation where some players make coordinated tactical movements (see In-depth analysis n.6).

So-called **"team tactics"** refers to the situation where coordinated tactical movements are made by the team as a whole (see In-depth analysis n.7).

To help the players achieve maximum tactical performance, the positions of the players on the field are determined by the **"systems"** or **"patterns of play"** (the "4-4-2", the "3-5-2", etc.).

By providing exact definitions of the players' positions and distances, the systems enable the development and the improvement of **schemes of play**.

Through consistent coaching, schemes enable the players "to agree in advance" on their movements during a match. Schemes are fundamental for purposes of the team realizing its tactical objective. At the same time, schemes are a concern for both players and coach because they are almost impossible to be carried out in the same way during the match as they were carried out in the coaching session. In fact, the presence of the opponents and of their countermeasures necessitates the application of numerous adaptive variations of the original schemes.

Therefore, in coaching, both the coach and the players must try to anticipate the opponents' countermeasures, and, as a consequence, develop possible responsive variations.

From this point of view, schemes do not limit the players' opportunity to express their personality; rather, they enable all those who have inventiveness to express their technical and tactical potential within the team's strategy.

Learning the technical skills

The learning process is never to be considered complete. Every level of ability that the player has achieved has room for further improvement. To enable further improvement, existing coaching methods must be reconsidered and supported by the following theoretical considerations.

During the game, the player applies his best technical and tactical potential and experience. By his cognitive **visual-perceptive** mechanism, he recognizes the movement of his teammates and of the opponents, as well as the effect of his actions on the play environment. Visual stimulation integrates with stimulation of **self-perception**. "Self-perception" takes "information from the inside" regarding the positions and movements of the body parts, and gives it to the brain. Then, with the cooperation of vestibular stimulation (which helps the body remain oriented in space during the movement), it enables the player to give a motor response. This response may be more or less suitable for the accomplishment of an objective, depending on the degree of technical skill that the player is able to use at that moment.

When in younger players their motor activity is not appropriate to the requirements of play, it must be corrected and improved in order to improve both individual and team performance.

The ability to make self-corrections **always** implies that the player must become aware of his mistake (cortical mechanism) which, if **emphasized** by the coach, enables the player to understand **what** mistake he has made and **where**.

The player can become aware of his mistake by recognizing that he has not done what he **intended** to do (for example, "I shot too high", "my poor pass created problems for my teammate", etc.). This is an easy and immediate way to check one's actions.

Otherwise, the player can analyze the stimulation that comes from his body (for example, "my body was off balance when I took that shot", "my supporting foot was not in the proper position", "I kicked the ball too much with the outside of the foot", etc.). Unless the coach uses a suitable coaching method, this other way to check one's action is not very likely to be found in younger players.

Finally, after the mistake has been pointed out, the coach must teach a consistent solution. Usually he corrects the mistake verbally, which most of the time has irrelevant results. Alternatively, he may suggest individual skills exercises, conducted either in pairs or in a group, which are characterized by requiring the player to **focus** on himself, that is, on how he must make a certain movement (for example, "keep your upper body tilted forward", "keep your knee over the ball", "the foot should be placed outward", etc.).

We think that the problem related to the coaching and the correction of technical skills should be dealt with in yet a different way, with a closer reference to Cognitive Sciences.

Our proposal

Our method emphasizes the player's ability to visually perceive the result of every action he takes. This enables him to correct possible mistakes by making motor adjustments of his own.

Specific exercise should be used only if the player, after many attempts, does not independently correct his movement. These exercises, by using a more controlled and analytical kind of movement, help the player to analyze the position and movement of his body parts.

Based on the theoretical principles that we have explained, we suggest that the development or the improvement of the technical skills should be carried out through four different kinds of exercises:

- **functional exercises,**
- **pre-situation exercises,**
- **situation exercises,**

in which the peculiar aspect is visual-motor check, and

- **bio-mechanical exercises,**

which are characterized by checking self-perceptive stimulation.

Functional exercises

In these exercises, the accomplishment of the pre-established objective is more important than the quality of the technical movement. The coach must be clear about the objective that the player must accomplish.

For example, a player can be asked to kick the ball high, toward the part of the goal which is on the right of the goalkeeper (this **intention** will be checked at the end of the action) by kicking the ball with the inside of the instep of his right foot (**way to carry out the movement**).

In this functional exercise the check is on whether or not the player addressed the ball toward the place required by the coach. If it is not, the coach must **not** correct the way in which the movement has been carried out (the balance of the body, the position of the foot, etc.). Rather, he must ask the player to keep on trying to accomplish the pre-established objective.

Let us consider now the way in which the coach should conduct the exercise.

The coach and the trainer should organize their exercise in a way that provides for it to be carried out in the context of small groups (2 to 6 players). This permits the players to benefit from numerous consecutive repetitions and to **develop motor adjustments on their own**, while being supported by advice such as "**try** to make the trajectory of the ball higher/lower", "**try** to kick the ball with a tighter/lob trajectory", etc.

If, after a certain number of sessions, the coach notices a sufficiently consistent achievement of the objective, this shows that the player is acquiring the style to develop that ability. It will be definitively achieved when, during the match, the player consistently applies what he has learned.

On the other hand, if the player does not show that he can consistently accomplish the pre-established objective, the coach should then have him carry out bio-mechanical exercises.

Bio-mechanical exercises

These exercises are characterized by a self-perceptive analysis of one's own body. They are used to make the player better understand the **reason for technical mistakes** which occur during the functional exercises.

Pre-situation exercises

The use of pre-situation exercises is helpful for purposes of making the technical skills developed in a functional and/or bio-mechanical context useful for actual competition.

These exercises are similar to functional exercises in the way they are performed, but are characterized by an environmental context which is more similar to that of a real match. For example, the players have more complex tasks which they must execute in a sequence, such as passing to a teammate, shooting at goal or solving some simple situations against opponents (who can be either passive or semi-active). Opponents are used to increase the level of difficulty of the exercise.

Situation exercises

The objective of these exercises is the improvement of both technical and athletic skills (special physical conditioning - SPC). Here, the intensity of the play is similar to the one experienced in a real match, or even higher. We suggest "match exercises" and "theme play" matches.

The practical method

Before dealing with the coaching of some fundamental technical elements, we think it is important to underline the importance of getting young players to practice those exercises that can be useful for **developing awareness of the body-ball relationship**. Among them, we suggest as an example those aimed at developing the ability to dribble and touch the ball.

Juggling the ball
◆ **Functional exercises**
The juggling must be carried out with various parts of the body and must accomplish pre-established objectives.

- juggling the ball up and down;
- juggling the ball up and down in narrow spaces;
- juggling the ball up and down while walking along an easy circuit;
- juggling the ball up and down while walking along a difficult circuit;
- juggling the ball in conditions of unstable balance;
- juggling the ball while running,
- competition to see who can juggle the ball more times in the way suggested by the coach;
- competition to try to juggle the ball as many times as possible in a pre-established time.

◆ **Bio-mechanic exercises**
Abilities must be improved by analytic exercises focusing on one part of the body:

- with alternate feet (with the instep, with the inside or the outside of the foot);
- with one foot;
- with the foot and the thigh;
- with the foot and the head;

- using the chest and the shoulders;
- alternating the variables.

◆ **Pre-situation exercises**

The ball must be received and controlled while juggling it; then, with the next touch, the ball must be passed to a teammate or a shot must be taken:

- receiving the ball with the head and then passing or shooting with the right and the left foot;
- receiving the ball with the chest and then passing or shooting with the right and the left foot;
- receiving the ball with the thigh or the knee and then passing or shooting with the right and the left foot;
- receiving the ball with the foot and then passing or shooting with a header;
- receiving the ball with the foot and then passing or shooting with the right and the left foot;
- the same exercises must be carried out with a semi-active opponent who disrupts the action.

Touching the ball

The player must focus on the result of the impact between his foot and the ball.

He must not make regular passes or take regular shots at goal. He must touch the ball in different ways, each of which he can then use to make a particular kind of pass or take a particular kind of shot.

◆ **Functional exercises**

Check the effect of the touch of the foot on the ball:

- low-ground ball which spins either forward, counterclockwise or clockwise;
- high ball which does not spin, or which spins counterclockwise, clockwise or backward;

◆ **Bio-mechanic exercises**

Consider the coordination of the movement, the position of the feet, the smoothness of the movement, the angle of the body, etc.

◆ **Pre-situation exercises**

Make cross-passes with inward spin or with outward spin, with an opponent disrupting the action.

Try to get the ball past the goalkeeper's reach, make lobs.

Dribbling the ball

◆ **Functional exercises**

The action must be quick, coordinated and well-paced:

- while **walking**, dribble the ball forward at a certain pace, passing the ball from one foot to the other;
- while **walking**, dribble the ball straight along a narrow corridor at a certain pace;
- while **walking**, dribble the ball forward following a hypothetical wide winding line at a certain pace;
- while **walking**, dribble the ball forward at a certain pace while slaloming through wide-spaced cones;
- while **running**, dribble the ball forward following a hypothetical wide winding line. As the ability improves, the speed of performance must be increased.
- while **running**, dribble the ball forward while slaloming through wide-spaced small poles arranged along the same line (then, the arrangement of the small poles should be wide-spaced and off-set, narrow-spaced and along the same line, narrow-spaced and offset). Here too, as the ability improves, the speed of performance must be increased.

◆ **Bio-mechanic exercises**

Depending on the deficiencies noticed in the previous exercises, more analytic exercises are carried out using:

- the inside of the foot;
- the outside of the foot;
- the sole of the foot;
- alternation of the variables.

◆ **Pre-situation exercises**

Dribbling the ball with the intention of accomplishing a further objective, such as passing the ball to a teammate, shooting at goal, dribbling the ball past an opponent, etc.;

Dribbling the ball while, for example, an opponent feints the tackle or feints his positioning along the path of the player's movement, in order to disrupt the dribbling.

Passing the ball

♦ Functional exercises

The objective is the precision of the result. The various parts of the foot should be used, as well as some other parts of the body:

- **From a dead ball position**: low-ground, high, short and long passes to a teammate who is **in a stand-by position**; then to a teammate who **comes toward the ball** from varying directions; finally to a teammate who **moves away from the ball** in varying directions;

- **With a low rolling ball coming from any direction**: low, high, short and long passes to a teammate who **is in a stand-by position**; then to a teammate who **comes toward the ball** from various directions; finally to a teammate who **moves away from the ball** toward various directions;

- **With a bouncing or high ball coming from any direction**: high, short and long passes to a teammate who is **in a stand-by position**; then to a teammate who **comes toward the ball** from varying directions; finally to a teammate who **moves away from the ball** in varying directions.

Variations

With a teammate placed at a short, middle and long distance:

- high passes: the ball must reach the teammate without touching the ground;
- high passes: the ball must reach the teammate after one or two bounces on the ground;

♦ Bio-mechanic exercises

The following exercises can be carried out if a certain difficulty is noticed in the performance of the previous exercises:

-make a pass, kicking a dead or rolling ball with:
- ❏ the inside of the foot;
- ❏ the outside of the foot;
- ❏ the inside of the instep;
- ❏ the tip of the foot;
- ❏ the heel.

- make a pass, kicking a bouncing or high ball with:
- ❏ the inside of the foot;
- ❏ the outside of the foot;
- ❏ the inside of the instep;
- ❏ the chest;

❑ the head;
❑ the knee.

◆   **Pre-situation exercises**
The same exercises recommended above can also be carried out with the addition of the following:
- **a short time** allowed for performance, to avoid pressure from an opponent;
- **a disrupting opponent**, who plays in semi-active marking.

Receiving the ball
◆   **Functional exercises**
The control of the ball is carried out with the foot, the thigh, the chest and the head. In these exercises, the player (either moving or in stand-by position) must receive and control balls from the right, from the left and from behind. These balls can be slow or fast, high, middle-height, low, bouncing, spinning, even lobs etc.

◆   **Bio-mechanic exercises**
Practice the way in which the ball is received when using:
❑ the inside of the foot, when receiving a low, middle-height or high ball;
❑ the inside of the foot, when the ball is received just after bouncing;
❑ the inside of the foot, when the player is running;
❑ the outside of the foot;
❑ the instep;
❑ the sole of the foot;
❑ the chest;
❑ the thigh.

◆   **Pre-situation exercises**
In these exercises:
- the reception of the ball is followed by other tasks, such as guided control of the ball toward a space free from opponents, dribbling, passes, protection of the ball, shots, etc.;
- the ball is controlled while an opponent disrupts the player's action.

Shooting

◆ **Functional exercises**

First with one foot, then with the other, the player tries to achieve his intention:

- **From a dead ball position**, he must take low, middle-height, high, central, rightward and leftward shots, alternating the combinations.
- **With a rolling ball moving away or coming from any direction**, he must take low, middle-height, high, central, rightward and leftward shots, with various combinations.
- **With a high ball moving away or coming from any direction**, he must take shots to the center, right and left on the volley.

◆ **Bio-mechanic exercises**

To correct the technical skills, practice shooting as follows:

- with the inside of the foot (not a powerful, but a precise shot);
- with the instep;
- with the lower part of the instep;
- with inward spin;
- with outward spin;
- with the tip of the foot.

In addition, check the following:

- the way in which the player takes the run-up;
- the position and the distance from the ball of the supporting foot;
- the zone of the foot that impacts the ball and the point of impact on the ball;
- after kicking, the leg must continue its movement smoothly and in a coordinated way.

◆ **Pre-situation exercises**

These exercises require the presence of the goalkeeper.

- shooting at goal **while an opponent** disrupts the action from in front, from behind, or from the right or from the left;
- shooting from different distances, trying to wrong-foot the goalkeeper (individual tactics);
- shooting after choosing the most useful technical way of kicking the ball to beat the goalkeeper's challenge.

Heading the ball

* **Functional exercises**

With the ball coming from any direction, carry out the following:

- **a defensive header** while **keeping the feet on the ground,** sending the ball forward, sideways, behind or toward an unmarked teammate;
- **an offensive header** while **keeping the feet on the ground:** the offensive header must result in a high, bouncing, shot at goal to the left and right.
- **an offensive header** while **keeping the feet on the ground,** making a pass to any pre-established direction;
- **a defensive header** while **jumping,** sending the ball forward, sideways, behind or toward an unmarked teammate;
- **an offensive header** while **jumping:** the offensive header must result in a high, bouncing shot at goal to the left and right.
- **an offensive header** while **jumping,** making a pass to any pre-established direction.

* **Bio-mechanic exercises**

In younger players, technical mistakes in headers are quite common. These mistakes are usually the result of the movements before the header (run-up, take-off, aerial phase), as the younger players have not completely developed the kind of strength that is necessary to carry out such a complex technical movement which closely depends on physical-athletic abilities.

Headers should be practiced as follows:

- with feet on the ground, head the ball forward;
- with feet on the ground, head the ball by a 90-degree rotation of the head to the left or to the right;
- with feet on the ground, head the ball by a 180-degree rotation of the head to the left or to the right;
- jumping, taking off on both feet, head the ball forward;
- jumping, taking off on the left or on the right foot, head the ball forward;
- jumping, taking off on the left foot, head the ball by a 90-degree rotation of the body to the left;
- jumping, taking off on the right foot, head the ball by a 90-degree rotation of the body to the right;
- head the ball by grazing it;
- head the ball with the back of the head.

♦ **Pre-situation exercises**

The same exercises recommended as above can be carried out with the addition of an opponent who disrupts the player in the phase before the header (during the run-up) or during the performance of the header.

Tackles
♦ **Functional exercises**

These exercises concern the possible ways of **facing an opponent** frontally, sideways or with the help of a shoulder, with the purpose of stealing the ball away from him or of preventing him from taking a defensive or an offensive action.

♦ **Bio-mechanic exercises**

These exercises aim at improving the orientation and the balance of the body, the position of the legs, the speed at which to approach the opponent, the movement of the foot used to steal the ball, etc.

♦ **Pre-situation exercises**

These exercises are meant to solve two problems:
- **Where** to tackle, considering the opponent's position on the field;
- **When** to tackle, in order to choose the best time.

Dribbling the ball past an opponent
♦ **Functional exercises**

Dribbling the ball past an opponent is quite a complex technical skill: its success depends on having already developed other abilities, such as control of the ball, feints, balance, and the ability to accurately assess the opponent's weaknesses so as to be able to successfully exploit these weaknesses in order to beat him on the left or on the right.

The exercises include numerous ways to beat an opponent, using various techniques as well as the element of "surprise".

The successful development of the ability to dribble the ball past an opponent depends on the opponent's ability to **defend by degrees**: he can be asked to place himself on the player's path of movement without taking any further action (passive defense) or to take action without aggressiveness (semi-active defense).

♦   **Bio-mechanic exercises**

There are some analytic exercises involving active and passive feints, which can be used to help the player focus on the controlled movement of his own body parts.

♦   **Pre-situation exercises**

As the player's ability improves, the opponent is required to participate in a passive way or to take action in a semi-active way.

In addition to trying to dribble the ball past the opponent facing him, the player tries to find space in front of himself in order to shoot, or to attract a second opponent to himself and thus unmark a teammate.

Final coaching notes

To further improve the technical aspect, and at the same time tactical cooperation, it is useful to introduce some synthesizing exercises in which the players can be involved globally.

One game, various objectives

The players can be asked to play a small sided game (6 on 6, 5 on 5 etc.), trying to accomplish some of the following objectives, which may be changed in the different sessions:

- warming up;
- using a certain technique to improve passing;
- focusing on cooperation between the teammate with the ball and other teammates who support him;
- placing pressure on the opponent with the ball;
- shooting at goal in a certain way.

Various games, one objective

6 to 8 different games can be organized, in which there is one common objective; for example, only one way to make passes, or to receive the ball, or to shoot, or only one tactical objective, etc.

Planning a typical coaching session

The coaching session must be considered as the basic operating unit. A typical coaching session includes the following phases:

- an **activation phase** which includes warming-up, pre-athletic exercises and general play exercises;

- a **technical-tactical phase**;
- a **phase of play**.

The activation phase

Of course there is no standardized warm-up. The physiological reasons that justify warm-up exercises are to increase body temperature, to stimulate enzymatic activities and metabolic reactions as well as energy systems, blood flow and availability of oxygen in the blood, and finally to decrease the situations of muscle contraction.

There are many factors that influence the form of this important phase of the coaching session: external temperature, the relationship between temperature and air humidity, the specific objective of the next activity, the physical build of the players, and whether the warm-up is before a coaching session or before a match.

As opposed to adults, young players do not need sophisticated warm-ups: it is enough for them to carry out a not too intense activity which, in a few minutes, increases their body temperature and their heart and breathing rate.

Therefore, games of movement are to be preferred. It is better to know many, so that this first phase of the coaching session can always be varied and interesting. Games, with or without the ball, meet the needs of effective activation when they involve all the players at the same time.

Therefore, a coach should suggest activities that involve the whole team rather than only a limited number of players.

Another thing to avoid is letting the players carry out individual skills exercises in the warm-up phase for a long time. Especially with younger players, these activities must be planned and carried out in other phases of the coaching session.

Also, while it may be carried out for a few minutes with adults, with younger players jogging should be avoided as a warm-up exercise because it is not a very motivating activity; it tends to dampen the response of the nervous system instead of stimulating a lively response.

In the activation phase, **pre-athletic** exercises should be carried out to accomplish various objectives.

◆   **Activation of the muscles of the arms and of the upper body**
The exercises for **the arms** include:
- throws (quick movements with outstretched arms);
- pushes (quick movements, from a flexed to an outstretched position);

- extensions (slow movements, from a flexed to an outstretched position);
- abductions (movements in which the arms move away from the body);
- adductions (movements in which the arms get closer to the body);
- outward rotations (outward movements around the longitudinal axis);
- inward rotations (inward movements around the longitudinal axis);
- circling with outstretched arms (movements with the shoulder joint acting as a fulcrum);
- flexing (movements from an outstretched to a flexed position with a non-supporting arm);
- bending (movements from an outstretched to a flexed position with a supporting arm).

The exercises for **the upper body** include:

- forward and sideways flexing;
- rotations to the right and left;
- flexing-rotations to the right and left;
- flexing-extensions;
- circling;
- exercises for the abdomen muscles;
- exercises for the back muscles.

♦   **Coordination strength in the legs**

In all the exercises, an objective is to teach jumping technique, enabling the player to improve the acceleration phase of the run.

In jumping, the legs must stretch in a coordinated way in order to make the thrust effective. Especially in multi-jumps, it is important to pay attention to the contact of the foot with the ground: the contact must be with the whole sole of the foot, not just with the heel or with the front part of the foot.

The number of jumps per exercise, or in the whole session, must not be too high. If sprints are included, it is important to consider that the first acceleration thrusts are maximum impulses of strength, therefore they demand the same muscle effort as jumps.

From the point of view of planning, it is possible to prepare sequences such as the following, according to the difficulty of performance:

1. All kinds of hops with outstretched legs, paying attention to the cushioning movement and the rapid thrust of the feet.

2. Single vertical jumps with the feet parallel to each other, with no interruption between the end of the bending and the beginning of the next thrust. The jumps can be made even without counter movement, using only the concentric phase of muscle contraction. In this case, the exercise starts with the legs bent at a 90 degree angle.

3. Vertical multiple jumps (no more than 3-5), paying attention to the pace of the movement and to the complete outstretching of the legs after the thrust.

4. Horizontal single jumps with the feet parallel to each other. Also this kind of jump can be taken without countermovement. Horizontal jumps are more difficult than vertical jumps, since the player has more difficulty in completely extending the legs in the phase of the thrust.

5. Horizontal multiple jumps (no more than 3-5), with the feet parallel to each other. Considerable attention should be given to the technique of the performance, as the younger players tend not to complete the thrust and to bend the legs as soon as the feet have left the ground.

6. Short alternating jumps (with a more upward than forward thrust), paying attention to the coordination between the trust of one leg and the bending forward movement of the other, as well as making sure that the entire sole of the foot contacts the ground (maximum 10 jumps in a row for each series of jumps).

7. Long alternating jumps (with a thrust aimed at landing as far forward as possible), making sure to completely stretch out the leg that is behind and that the other leg is bent and far forward (triple and quintuple jump).

8. Run with jumps. This is the most important activity, as it is the intermediate learning phase between the jumps and the run.

Among the various kinds of jumps, we advise against repeated jumps on the same foot, as their correct performance requires high levels of strength and coordination which are difficult to find in younger players. In addition, in order to develop muscle plyometric qualities, the coaching plan can include jumps over low hurdles (no more than five hurdles) and vertical jumps after jumping down from a bench.

In order to assess the level of stretching ability reached, after the execution of a plyometric exercise, it useful to carry out 5/10-yard sprints from a standing start. During the sprint, the players should make sure to push with strength using the leg on the ground, even though at first, in order to lengthen their time in the air, the younger players will tend to slow the rate of the steps. In time, when coordination in jumps and sprints improves, the quickness of the steps will increase and a real increase in the acceleration ability over very short distances will occur.

◆   **Improvement of flexibility**

In order to develop flexibility, we refer you to the principles contained in our previous book ; however, we do not recommend passive stretching exercises.

If the muscle ability of the players is already sufficient, the objective of the activity of muscle stretching will be to maintain the proper:

- forward flexibility of the spine from a standing position;
- frontal wide-apart movement of the legs in a sitting position;
- ability to maintain a hurdle-shaped position from a sitting position, without the help of the hands.

◆   **The technical-tactical phase**

The recommend exercises to be carried out are as follows:

- **With a time deadline**

For example: a tournament with 3/4-player teams, with very short play time (3 or 4 minutes).

- **With more verbal information**

The player with the ball must try to follow the directions that are given verbally to him by his closest teammate or by the coach.

- **With less verbal information**

In this case his teammates and the coach must remain silent.

- **With less visual information**

For example, two teams play a small-sided match wearing shirts of the same color; or, in a specific exercise the players can be required to shoot at goal or to pass to a teammate without directly looking at the ball, but keeping the ball in their field of vision.

- **Changing tactical tasks**

During the play, team tactics can be changed (by changing the system of play, by applying zone play or man-marking play). The changes can be made compulsory in some pre-established zones of the field or maintained for some period of time.

The phase of play

Usually, a game concludes the coaching session.

We think that in soccer schools and in the youth sector the last part of the coaching session should include:

- **theme play** to **reinforce** the technical skills that the player has already developed . During the play, if necessary, the coach should guide the players with his voice to help them choose the best options and solutions;
- **unrestricted play,** by which the coach can **check** if the various abilities have become automatic in the players.

During the game the coach should not give advice, but take notes. If he notices some unsatisfactory technical or tactical movements, then that aspect should be the object of further work in the next sessions.

CHAPTER THREE
PRACTICAL EXERCISES

Introduction to Chapter Three,
by M. Oneto and G. Ferrera

Chapter three contains some practical exercises. From the various kinds of exercises suggested in this book, we have chosen **pre-situation exercises**, to give both trainers and coaches a more meaningful explanation of what we intend to express in this book.

Pre-situation exercises are a coaching means in between the phase of technical coaching and the phase of tactical coaching. They are complex activities, as they include combinations of specific technical movements which are also made more challenging by the presence of "opponents" that can be either passive or semi-active, according to what is needed. In addition, they involve any number of players, ranging from 3-5 to 8-10, who repeat the targeted fundamental movements a considerable number of times.

These exercises provide the opportunity to accomplish two objectives: the first is the improvement of the quality of coaching, due to the high number of repetitions executed in a way which is very similar to real match situations.

The second is the continuous improvement of the players' physical-athletic condition, as the neuro-motor training phase is developed in a context which is made difficult by the enduring effort determined by the players' repetitive actions.

The single exercises can be carried out both clockwise and counter-clockwise. This is important, as in this way the player must use both feet, alternately.

Other variations that influence the intensity of the exercises are the number of players involved and the distances between them. As we have said above, these are complex exercises, as the task that the players are required to perform is not limited to one; in fact, they are required to carry out a sequence of movements by applying various technical skills.

The function of the coach is fundamental, as he must advise, correct and support the players when he sees their difficulty.

EXERCISE 1

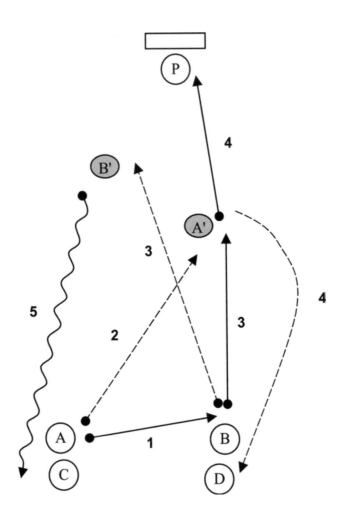

Technical objective

♦   SHOT AT GOAL
♦   PASSING THE BALL ON A TEAMMATE'S STRIDE
♦   RECEIVING
♦   DIAGONAL RUN

Description

Four (or more) players plus the goalkeeper (P) are involved.
A has the ball.

1 -   A makes a low-ground pass to B, who receives

2 -   A makes a diagonal run and moves to position A'

3 -   B makes a low-ground pass to A in position A', then runs to
            position B' to intercept a possible clearance from the goalkeeper

4 -   A shoots at goal and then lines up behind D

5 -   B dribbles the ball behind C

Next position

Player A goes to the position of player D
Player B goes to the position of player C

EXERCISE 2

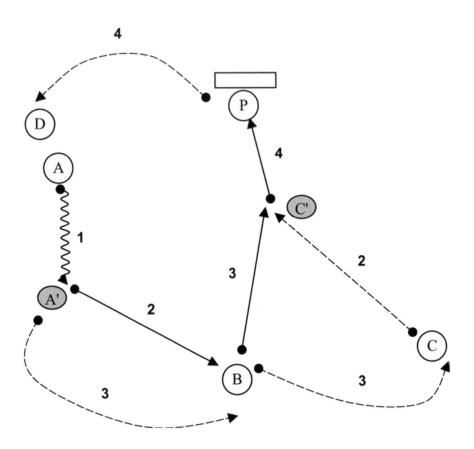

Technical objective
- SHOT AT GOAL
- LOW-GROUND PASS
- DIAGONAL RUN
- DRIBBLING THE BALL
- "PASS AND FOLLOW"

Description
Three groups of two (or more) players plus the goalkeeper (P) are involved.
A has the ball.

1 -   A dribbles the ball toward position A'

2 -   A makes a low-ground pass to B, while C makes a diagonal run to position C'

3 -   B passes to C in position C' and runs to the starting position of player C, while A runs to the starting position of player B

4 -   C shoots at goal, then takes the ball and lines up behind player D

Next position
Player A goes to the position of player B
Player B goes to the position of player C
Player C goes to the position of player A

EXERCISE 3

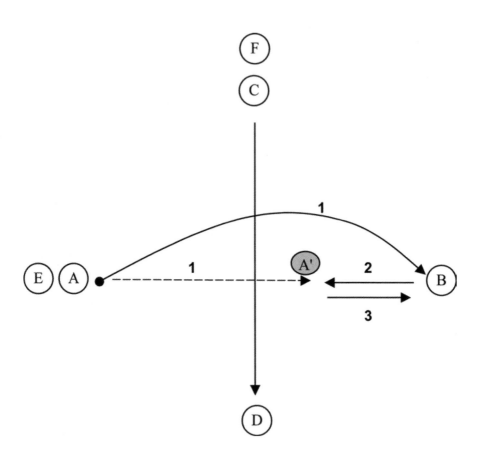

Technical objective

♦   LOW-GROUND PASS
♦   LOB PASS
♦   RECEIVING
♦   WALL PASS
♦   "PASS AND FOLLOW"

Description

Two groups of three (or more) players on opposite sides are involved.
A and C have the ball.

1 -   A makes a lob pass to B and moves toward him

2 -   B receives and passes back to A, who receives in position A'

3 -   A makes a pass on the volley to B, who then carries out the same exercise and at the end lines up behind player E

The exercise develops in the same way for the other group, except that the pass is a low-ground pass

Next position

Player A goes to the position of player B
Player B goes to the position of player E
Player C goes to the position of player D
Player D goes to the position of player F

EXERCISE 4

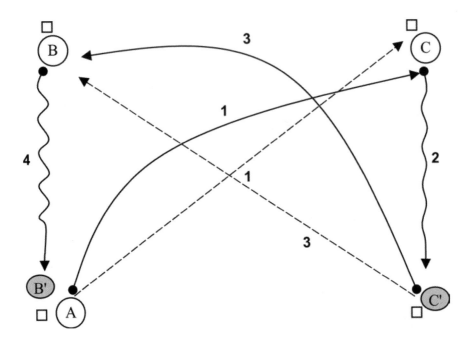

Technical objective

- ◆ LOB PASS
- ◆ GUIDED CONTROL
- ◆ DRIBBLING THE BALL
- ◆ "PASS AND FOLLOW"

Description

Three players are involved, each placed at one corner of a square (one corner is left free).
A has the ball.

1 -   A makes a lob pass to C and follows the ball

2 -   C receives with a guided control and dribbles the ball toward the free corner (position C')

3 -   C makes a lob pass to B and follows the ball

4 -   B receives with a guided control and dribbles the ball toward the free corner (now position B') to continue the exercise

Next position

Player A goes to the position of player C
Player C goes to the position of player B
Player B goes to the position of player A

EXERCISE 5

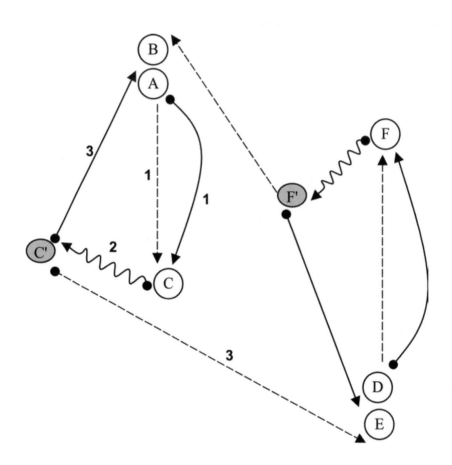

Technical objective

- LOB PASS
- GUIDED CONTROL
- DRIBBLING THE BALL
- "PASS AND FOLLOW"
- "PASS AND GO"

Description

Two groups of three (or more) players are involved.
A and D have a ball.

1 - A makes a lob pass to C and follows the ball

2 - C receives with a guided control toward the left and dribbles the ball to position C'

3 - C makes a low-ground pass to B, then runs to line up behind E

D, E and F do the exercise at the same time as A, B and C, but they guide the control of the ball toward the right

Next position

Player A goes to the position of player C
Player C goes to the position of player E
Player D goes to the position of player F
Player F goes to the position of player B

EXERCISE 6

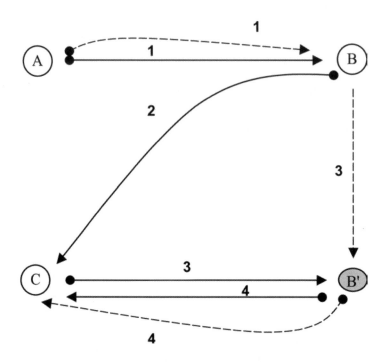

Technical objective

- "PASS AND FOLLOW"
- RECEIVING
- LOB PASS
- "PASS AND GO"

Description

Three players are involved, each placed at one corner of a square (one corner is left free).

A has the ball.

1 - A makes a low-ground pass to B and follows the ball

2 - B receives and makes a lob pass to C

3 - B moves to position B' to receive the return pass

4 - B makes a low-ground pass to C and follows the ball

C starts a new sequence by serving A

Next position

Player A goes to the position of player B

Player B goes to the position of player C

Player C goes to the position of player A

EXERCISE 7

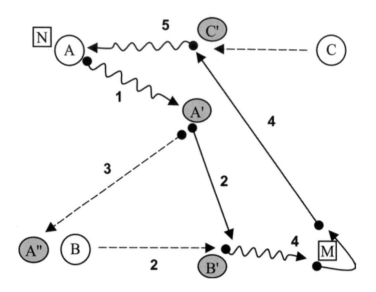

Technical objective

- DRIBBLING THE BALL
- PASS ON A TEAMMATE'S MOVEMENT
- RECEIVING
- FEINT AND DRIBBLING PAST AN OPPONENT

Description

Three (or more) players are involved, each placed at one corner of a square.

A has the ball.

1 - A dribbles the ball forward to position A'

2 - A makes a pass on the movement of player B, who receives in position B'

3 - A moves to position A" with a deviating run

4 - B dribbles the ball toward position M (free corner), makes a feint, dribbles the ball past a cone and makes a pass on the movement of player C who runs to receive in position C'

5 - C dribbles the ball toward position N (free corner) and continues the exercise

Next position

Player A goes to the position of player B
Player B goes to the position of player C
Player C goes to the position of player A

EXERCISE 8

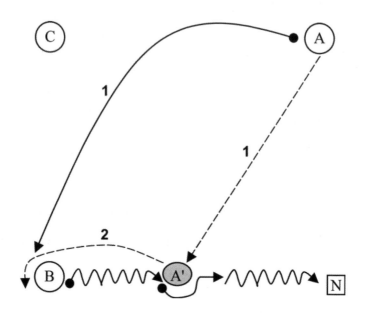

Technical objective

- ◆ DRIBBLING THE BALL
- ◆ LOB PASS
- ◆ GUIDED CONTROL
- ◆ FEINT AND DRIBBLING

Description

Three players are involved, each placed at one corner of a square (one corner is left free).

A has the ball.

1 - A makes a lob pass to B and runs to position A' to defend

2 - B receives, dribbles the ball past A (who is in position A') and, while he reaches position N (free corner), player A leaves his position and goes to the starting position of player B

3 - B continues the exercise by passing to C

Next position

Player A goes to the position of player B
Player B goes to the position of player C
Player C goes to the position of player A

EXERCISE 9

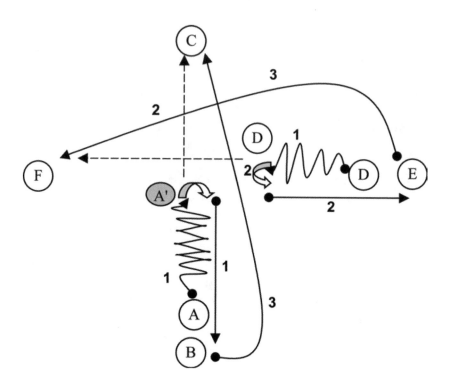

Technical objective
- DRIBBLING THE BALL
- FEINT
- "PASS AND GO"
- LOW-GROUND AND LOB PASS
- RECEIVING

Description
Two groups of three (or more) players are involved.
A and D have a ball.

1 - A dribbles the ball toward position A', makes a feint with a change of direction and then makes a low-ground pass to B

2 - After making the pass, A runs to line up behind player C

3 - B receives and makes a lob pass to C, who receives and continues the exercise. D, E and F carry out the exercise in the same way

Next position
Player A goes to the position of player C
Player D goes to the position of player F
Player C goes to the position of player B
Player F goes to the position of player E

EXERCISE 10

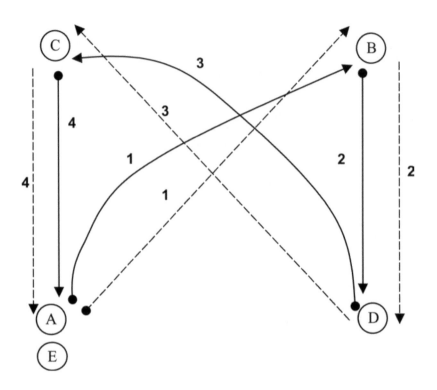

Technical objective

* LOB PASS
* RECEIVING
* LOW-GROUND PASS
* "PASS AND FOLLOW"

Description
Five (or more) players are involved, each placed at one corner of a square. A has the ball.

1 - A makes a lob pass to B and follows the ball

2 - B receives, makes a low-ground pass to D and follows the ball

3 - D receives, makes a lob-pass to C and follows the ball

4 - C receives and makes a low-ground pass to E

Next position
Player A goes to the position of player B
Player B goes to the position of player D
Player D goes to the position of player C
Player C goes to the position of player A

EXERCISE 11

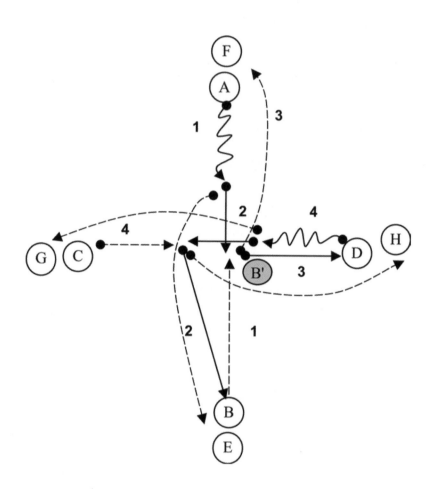

Technical objective

- DRIBBLING THE BALL
- LOW-GROUND PASS
- "PASS AND FOLLOW"
- RECEIVING

Description

Four groups of two (or more) players on opposite sides are involved.
A has the ball.

1 - A dribbles the ball forward while B goes toward him (to position B')

2 - A makes a low-ground pass to B and runs to line up behind E

3 - B makes a pass to D and runs to line up behind F

4 - D continues the exercise and C moves toward him

Next position

Player A goes to the position of player B
Player B goes to the position of player A
Player D goes to the position of player C
Player C goes to the position of player D

EXERCISE 12

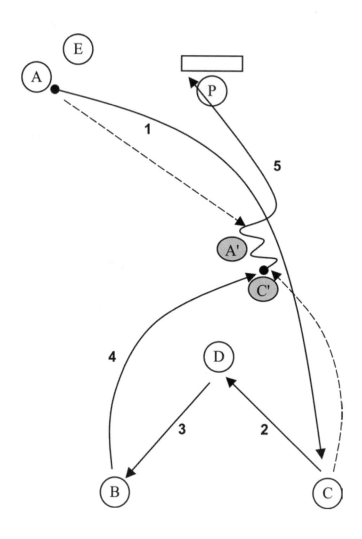

Technical objective

* SHOT AT GOAL
* PASS
* FEINT AND DRIBBLING THE BALL PAST AN OPPONENT

Description

This exercise must be carried out from the right and from the left. Five players plus the goalkeeper (P) are involved.
A has the ball.

1 - A makes a lob pass to C, and runs to position A' to defend

2 - C makes a pass on the volley to D

3 - D makes a pass on the volley to B

4 - B passes to C who receives in position C', then dribbles the ball past A (who is in position A') and shoots at goal

5 - E restarts the exercise when C shoots at goal

Next position

Player A goes to the position of player D
Player D goes to the position of player B
Player B goes to the position of player C
Player C goes to the position of player E

EXERCISE 13

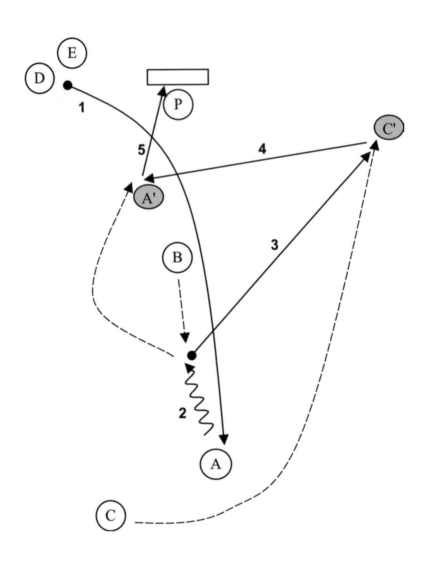

Technical objective

- SHOT AT GOAL
- PASS
- OVERLAPPING RUN
- DRIBBLING THE BALL

Description

Five (or more) players plus the goalkeeper (P) are involved.
D has the ball.

1 - D makes a lob pass to A

2 - A receives and C carries out an overlapping run toward position C'; A dribbles the ball toward B who attacks him

3 - When attacked by B, A passes to C who is in position C' after carrying out the overlapping run

4 - C passes to A in position A'

5 - A receives and shoots at goal

Next position

Player A goes to the position of player E
Player C goes to the position of player B
Player B goes to the position of player A
Player D goes to the position of player C

EXERCISE 14

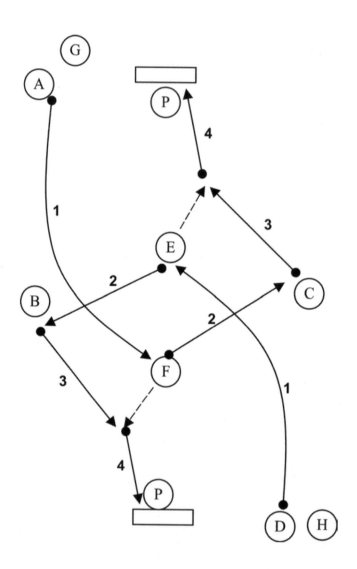

Technical objective
- SHOT AT GOAL
- PASS

Description
Eight (or ten) players plus two goalkeepers (P) are involved.
A and D have a ball.

1 - A and D make a lob pass to F and E

2 - F and E make a pass on the volley to B and C

3 - B and C make a return pass on the volley to F and E

4 - F and E shoot at goal

When F and E shoot at goal, H and G restart the exercise

Next position
Player A goes to the position of player B
Player B goes to the position of player F
Player F goes to the position of player H
Player D goes to the position of player C
Player C goes to the position of player E
Player E goes to the position of player G

EXERCISE 15

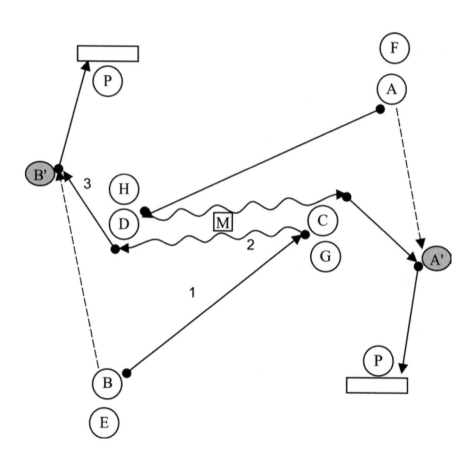

Technical objective

◆   SHOT AT GOAL

◆   PASS

◆   FEINTS AND DRIBBLING THE BALL

Description

Eight players plus two goalkeepers (P) are involved.
A and B have the ball.

1 -   A and B pass to C and D

2 -   C and D dribble the ball toward each other and make a feint when
       they reach point M

3 -   C and D pass to B and A, who have followed the action and are
       respectively in positions B' and A' .

4 - A and B shoot at goal

Next position

Player A goes to the position of player C
Player D goes to the position of player A
Player C goes to the position of player B
Player B goes to the position of player C

EXERCISE 16

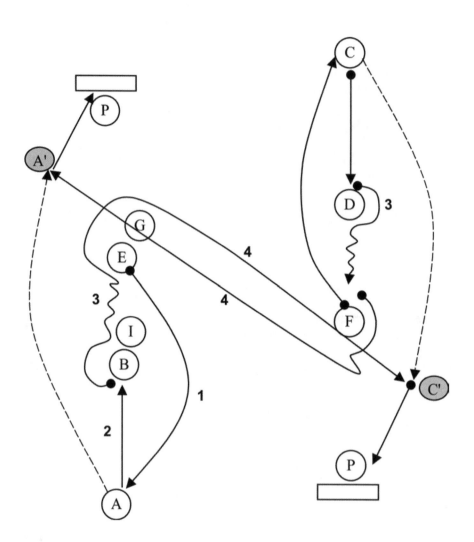

Technical objective

- SHOT AT GOAL
- PASS
- FEINTS AND DRIBBLING THE BALL

Description

Eight players plus two goalkeepers (P) are involved.
E and F have a ball.

1 - E passes to A; F passes to C

2 - A passes to B; C passes to D

3 - B and D receive, guiding the control of the ball, respectively, toward E and F to dribble the ball past them

4 - B and D make a long pass, respectively, to C and A, who receive in positions C' and A' and then shoot at goal

I and G take the place of B and F in the next repetition of the exercise.

Next position

After B has dribbled the ball past player E, the latter goes to the position of player A
After shooting, player A goes to the position of player I
After passing, player B goes to the position of player G

EXERCISE 17

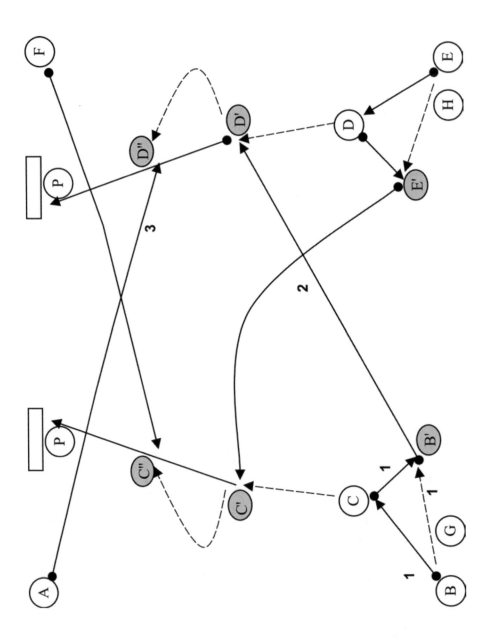

Technical objective

• SHOT AT GOAL

• PASS

Description

Eight (or ten) players plus two goalkeepers (P) are involved.
B and E have a ball.

1 - B passes to C and C returns him the ball in position B'

2 - In position B', B makes a low-ground pass to D who receives in position D' and shoots at goal

3 - Then D, in position D", receives a lob pass from A to take another shot

The same exercise is done by the players in the other positions.

From position E', E makes a lob pass to C in position C', and F makes a further pass to C in position C".

Next position

Player B goes to the position of player C
Player C goes to the position of player A
Player A goes to the position of player B

EXERCISE 18

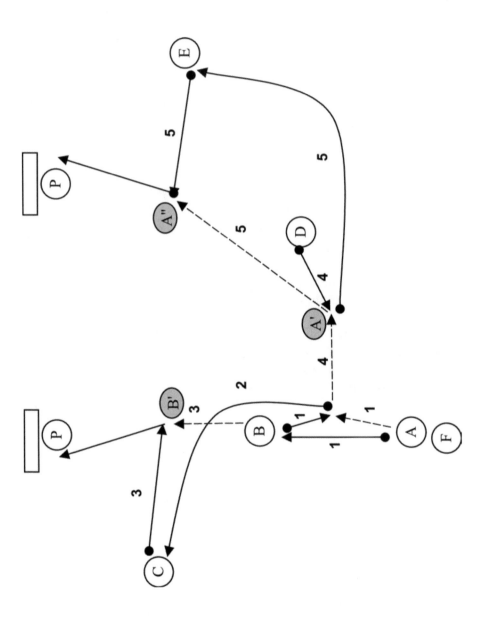

Technical objective

* ◆ SHOT AT GOAL
* ◆ PASS

Description

Six (or eight) players plus two goalkeepers (P) are involved.
A and D have a ball.

1 -   A passes to B and B returns him the ball

2 -   A makes a lob pass to C

3 -   C makes a pass on the volley to B in position B', and B shoots at goal

4 -   After passing to C, A runs to receive the pass from D

5 -   From position A', A passes to E, who returns him the ball on the volley toward position A", from which A shoots at the other goal

Next position

Player A goes to the position of player E
Player E goes to the position of player D
Player D goes to the position of player B
Player B goes to the position of player C
Player C goes to the position of player F

EXERCISE 19

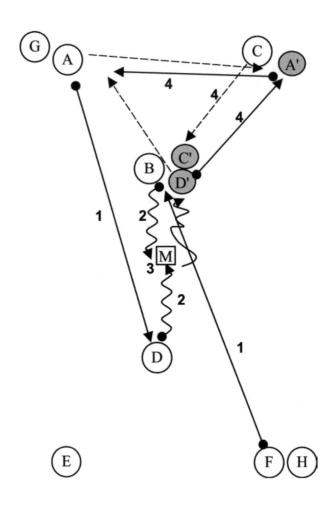

Technical objective

- PASS
- RECEIVING
- FEINT AND DRIBBLING THE BALL

Description

Eight players are involved.

The exercise should be carried out both to the left and to the right.

A and F have a ball.

1 - A passes to D and F passes to B

2 - B receives and dribbles the ball toward D, who dribbles the other ball toward B at the same time

3 - B and D make a feint and dribble the ball past each other in a semi-active way in position M

4 - D, in position D', makes a one-two pass (triangulation) with A, who runs to receive in position A', while C attacks D in position C'

The same exercise is carried out at the same time by E and F with B

Next position

Player A goes to the position of player C

Player B goes to the position of player F

Player D goes to the position of player A

Player C goes to the position of player B

Player F goes to the position of player E

EXERCISE 20

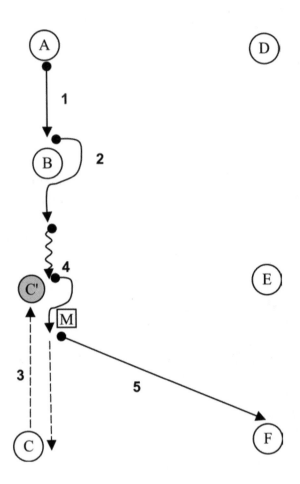

Technical objective

- PASS
- RECEIVING
- FEINT AND DRIBBLING THE BALL

Description

Six players are involved; they make clockwise and counterclockwise movements.

A has the ball.

1 -   A passes to B

2 -   B receives and dribbles the ball toward C

3 -   C runs toward B to tackle him in a semi-active way in position M

4 -   B makes a feint in position M and dribbles the ball past C

5 -   B passes to F

The same exercise is carried out at the same time by E, F and D

Next position

Player A and F remain in their positions
Player C goes to the position of player B
Player B goes to the position of player C
Player E goes to the position of player F
Player F goes to the position of player E

EXERCISE 21

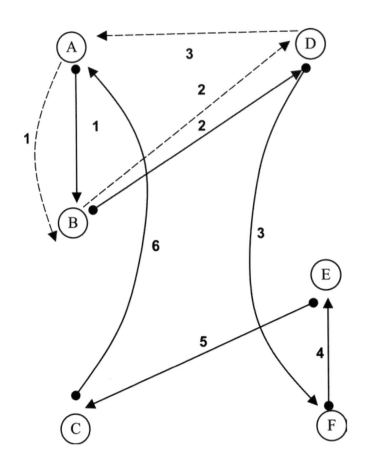

Technical objective

- ◆   LOW-GROUND AND LOB PASS
- ◆   "PASS AND FOLLOW"
- ◆   "PASS AND GO"

Description

Six players are involved; they make clockwise and counterclockwise movements.

A has the ball.

1 -   A makes a low-ground pass to B and follows the ball

2 -   B makes a low-ground pass to D and follows the ball

3 -   D makes a lob pass to F and goes to the position vacated by A

4 -   F makes a low-ground pass to E and follows the ball

5 -   E makes a low-ground pass to C and follows the ball

6 -   C makes a lob pass to A and goes to the position vacated by F

Next position

Player A goes to the position of player B
Player B goes to the position of player D
Player D goes to the position of player A
Player C goes to the position of player F
Player F goes to the position of player E
Player E goes to the position of player C

EXERCISE 22

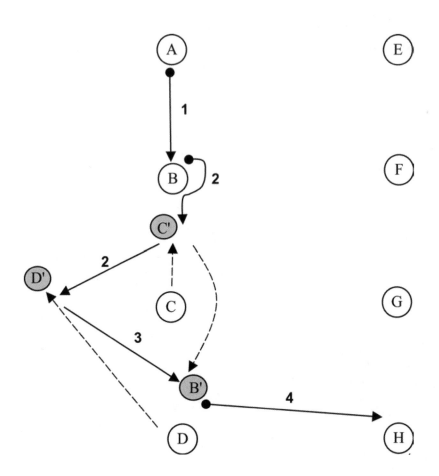

Technical objective

- PASS
- GUIDED CONTROL
- FEINT AND DRIBBLING THE BALL

Description

Eight players are involved. The positions are changed to make all the players carry out the circuit.

A has the ball.

1 - A makes a pass to B, who receives and dribbles the ball toward C

2 - When he is near position C', B feints to dribble the ball past C and instead serves D in position D'

3 - D passes to B in position B'

4 - B passes to H, who continues the exercise with the other players

Next position

Player A and player H maintain their positions
Player B goes to the position of player D
Player C goes to the position of player B
Player D goes to the position of player C
Player E goes to the position of player F
Player F goes to the position of player G
Player G goes to the position of player E

EXERCISE 23

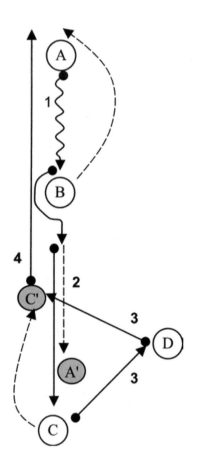

Technical objective

- PASS
- RECEIVING
- GUIDED CONTROL
- FEINT AND DRIBBLING THE BALL
- ONE-TWO PASS (TRIANGULATION)

Description

Four players are involved. The exercise must be carried out with triangulations both to the right and to the left.

A has the ball.

1 -   A dribbles the ball toward B, and then dribbles the ball past him

2 -   A passes to C, and runs to position A' to attack him

3 -   C receives and carries out a triangulation (one-two) with D

4 -   C receives the pass in position C', then passes to B who restarts the exercise with the other players

Next position

Player A goes to the position of player D
Player B goes to the position of player A
Player C goes to the position of player B
Player D goes to the position of player C

EXERCISE 24

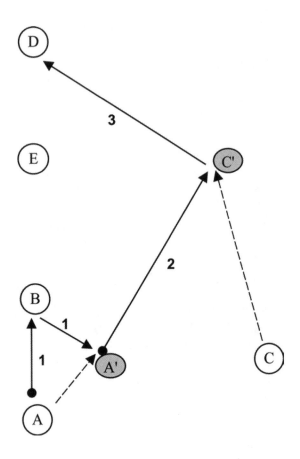

Technical objective
- SHORT AND LONG LOW-GROUND PASS ON THE
  TEAMMATE'S STRIDE
- RECEIVING

Description
Six (or eight) players are involved. They make clockwise and counterclock-wise movements.
A has the ball.

1 -   A passes to B, who returns the ball to him in position A'

2 -   A makes a low-ground pass to C in position C'

3 -   C makes a pass on the volley to D

The same exercise is then carried out by the other players.

The same exercise can also be carried out with a lob pass from D to F and from F to A.

Next position
Player A goes to the position of player C
Player C goes to the position of player E
Player B goes to the position of player A
Player D goes to the position of player F
Player F goes to the position of player B
Player E goes to the position of player D

EXERCISE 25

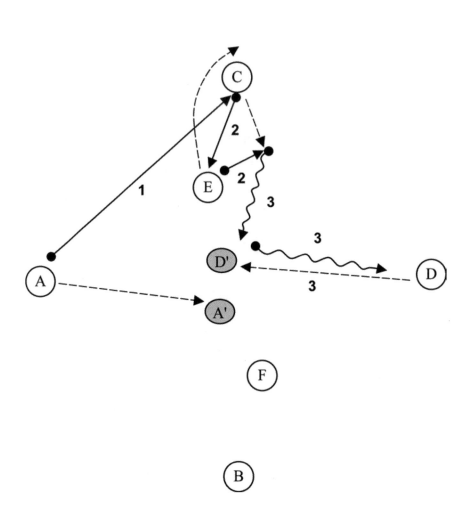

Technical objective

- PASS
- FEINT AND DRIBBLING THE BALL
- DRIBBLING THE BALL

Description

Eight (or ten) players are involved.
A and D have a ball.

1 - A passes to C and runs to position A' to defend

2 - C makes a triangulation on the volley with E and, after receiving the return pass, dribbles the ball toward D who runs to position D' to defend

3 - C makes a feint on D and dribbles the ball toward the position vacated by D to restart the exercise

The same exercise is then carried out by D, F and B.

Next position

Player A goes to the position of player F
Player B goes to the position of player A
Player C goes to the position of player D
Player D goes to the position of player E
Player E goes to the position of player C
Player F goes to the position of player B

EXERCISE 26

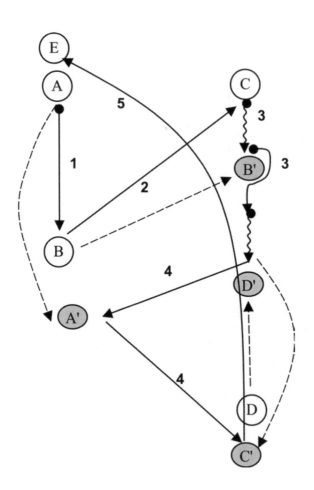

Technical objective
- LOW-GROUND AND LOB PASS
- "PASS AND FOLLOW" TRIANGULATION
- FEINT AND DRIBBLING THE BALL

Description
Five players are involved.
A has the ball.

1 - A passes to B and follows the ball

2 - B makes a low-ground pass to C and makes a diagonal run to attack him in position B'

3 - C dribbles the ball past B

4 - C makes a triangulation with A in position A' to beat D in position D'

5 - C makes a long lob pass to E

Next position
Player A goes to the position of player B
Player B goes to the position of player C
Player C goes to the position of player D
Player D goes to the position of player A

EXERCISE 27

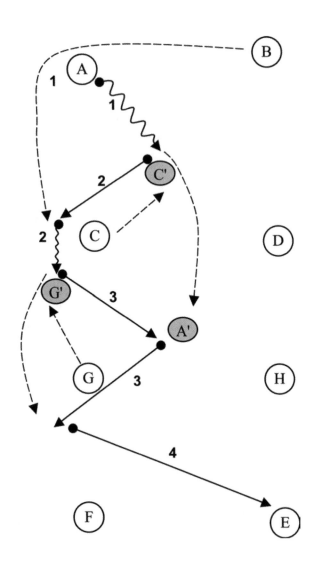

Technical objective
- DRIBBLING THE BALL
- OVERLAPPING RUN
- PASS
- TRIANGULATION

Description

Eight players are involved.
A has the ball.

1 - A dribbles the ball toward C in position C', while B makes an overlapping run

2 - A makes a low-ground pass to B, who dribbles the ball toward G in position G'

3 - B passes to A in position A', who returns the ball to him on the volley

4 - B makes a pass on the volley to E, who restarts the exercise with the other players

Next position

Player A goes to the position of player F
Player B goes to the position of player G
Player G goes to the position of player C
Player C goes to the position of player A

EXERCISE 28

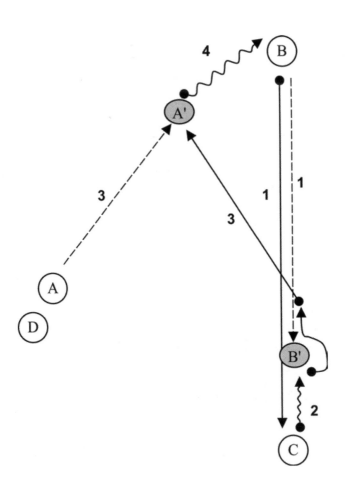

Technical objective
- PASSING THE BALL ON THE TEAMMATE'S STRIDE
- FEINT AND DRIBBLING THE BALL

Description
Four players are involved. The exercise is carried out both to the right and to the left.

B has the ball.

1 -   B passes to C and goes to position B' to tackle him

2 -   C receives, feints and dribbles the ball past B

3 -   C passes the ball to A on A's stride, and A receives in position A'

4 -   A dribbles the ball forward and restarts the exercise

Next position
Player A goes to the position of player B

Player B goes to the position of player C

Player C goes to the position of player A

EXERCISE 29

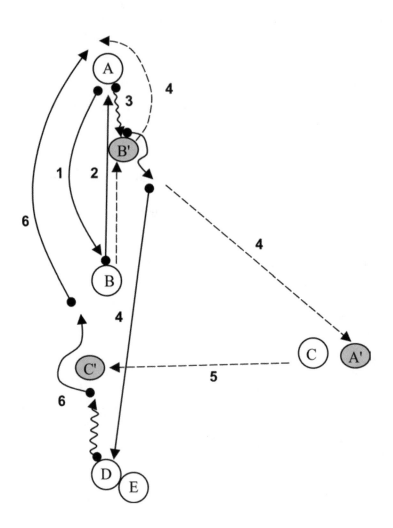

Technical objective
+ WALL PASS
+ FEINT AND DRIBBLING THE BALL
+ RECEIVING

Description
Five (or six) players are involved. The exercise is carried out both to the right and to the left.
A has the ball.

1 -   A makes a lob pass to B

2 -   B makes a pass to A on the volley, then runs to position B' to tackle him

3 -   A receives, dribbles the ball toward B and beats him with a feint, dribbling the ball past him

4 -   A passes to D and runs to position A' while B takes A's place

5 -   As soon as A passes to D, C carries out a diagonal run to tackle D in position C'

6 -   D dribbles the ball past C and makes a long pass to B to restart the exercise

Next position
Player A goes to the position of player C
Player B goes to the position of player A
Player C goes to the position of player D
Player D goes to the position of player B

EXERCISE 30

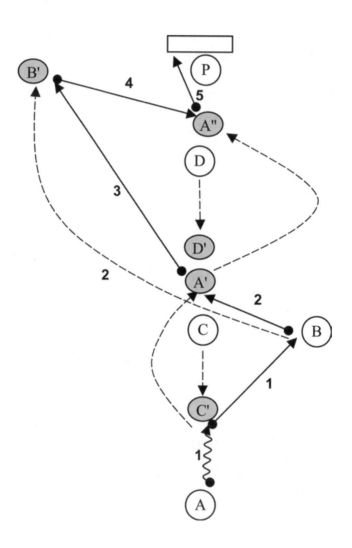

Technical objective

* TRIANGULATION
* "PASS AND GO"
* "PASS AND FOLLOW"
* SHOT AT GOAL

Description

Four (or eight) players are involved.
A has the ball.

1 - A dribbles the ball toward C, carries out a triangulation with B and receives the return pass in position A'

2 - B carries out a triangulation with A and runs to position B'

3 - A, in position A', passes to B in position B'

4 - B passes to A in position A"

5 - A shoots at goal from position A"

C and D tackle A in positions C' and D'

Next position

Player A goes to the position of player D
Player B goes to the position of player F
Player C goes to the position of player A
Player D goes to the position of player B

EXERCISE 31

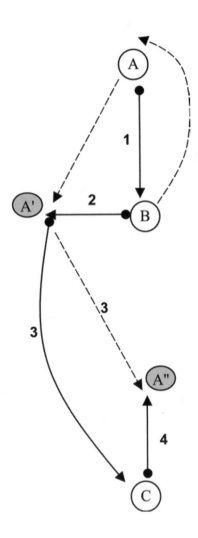

Technical objective
- ◆ LOB PASS AND LOW-GROUND PASS
- ◆ TRIANGULATION

Description
Three (or four) players are involved.
A has the ball.

1 - A passes to B

2 - B passes back to A in position A'

3 - A makes a lob pass to C and runs to position A"

4 - C receives and restarts the exercise with a pass to A in position A"

Next position
Player B goes to the position of player A
Player A goes to the position of player C
Player C goes to the position of player B

EXERCISE 32

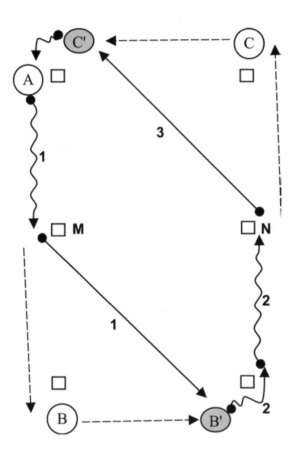

Technical objective

- DIAGONAL PASS TAKEN BY THE TEAMMATE IN STRIDE
- DRIBBLING THE BALL
- RECEIVING

Description

Three players are involved.

This exercise must be carried out both clockwise and counterclockwise.

Each player continues his run to reach the next position.

A has the ball.

1 -   A dribbles the ball toward a small cone (M) and, with the inside of the foot, passes to B, who runs to position B' to receive the ball

2 -   B dribbles the ball toward another small cone (N) and, with the inside of the foot, passes to C, who runs to position C' to receive the ball

3 -   After receiving, C continues the exercise by passing to A

Next position

Player A goes to the position of player B

Player B goes to the position of player C

Player C goes to the position of player A

EXERCISE 33

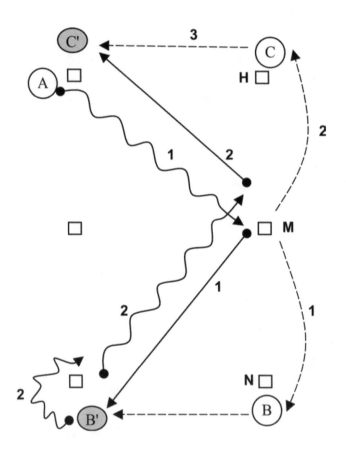

Technical objective

◆   DRIBBLING THE BALL

◆   PASS TAKEN BY THE TEAMMATE IN STRIDE

◆   RECEIVING

Description

Three players are involved.

This exercise must be carried out both clockwise and counterclockwise.

Each player continues his run to reach the next position.

A has the ball.

1 -   A dribbles the ball toward a small cone (M) and, with the inside of
the left foot, passes to B in position B', then A continues running
toward another small cone (N)

2 -   B dribbles the ball toward small cone M and, with the inside of
the right foot, passes to C in position C', then B continues his run
toward small cone H

3 -   After receiving, C continues the exercise from position A

Next position

Player A goes to the position of player B

Player B goes to the position of player C

Player C goes to the position of player A

EXERCISE 34

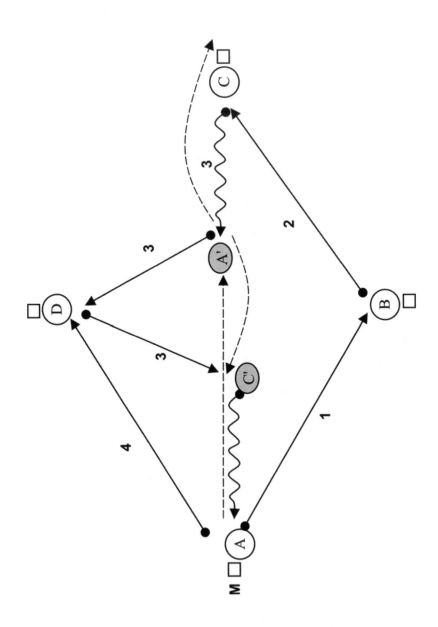

Technical objective

◆ PASS

◆ TRIANGULATION

◆ DRIBBLING THE BALL

Description

Four players are involved.

This exercise must be carried out both to the right and to the left.

A has the ball.

1 - A passes to B

2 - B makes a pass on the volley to C

3 - C dribbles the ball toward A, who runs to position A' to tackle C, and beats him because of a triangulation with D; C receives from D in position C' and dribbles the ball toward a small cone (M)

4 - C passes to D and D continues the exercise

Next position

Player A goes to the position of player C

Player D goes to the position of player B

Player B goes to the position of player D

Player C goes to the position of player A

EXERCISE 35

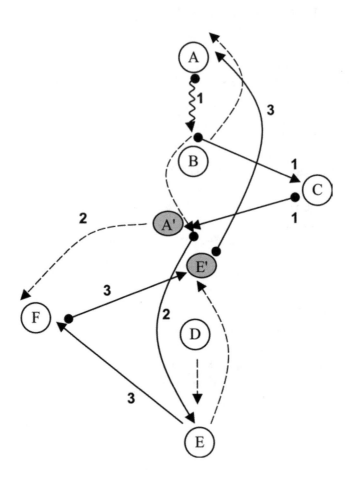

Technical objective
- DRIBBLING THE BALL
- TRIANGULATION
- LOB PASS
- PASS ON THE VOLLEY

Description
Six (or eight) players are involved.
This exercise must be carried out both to the right and to the left.
A has the ball.

1 - A dribbles the ball toward B and carries out a triangulation with C, who returns the ball to him in position A'

2 - A receives and makes a lob pass to E, then runs to position F

3 - E makes a pass on the volley to player F, then runs to position E' to receive the return pass and makes a lob pass to B, who has taken the place of player A

4 - B and D act as passive defenders

Next position
Player A goes to the position of player F
Player B goes to the position of player A
Player C goes to the position of player B
Player D goes to the position of player E
Player E goes to the position of player C
Player F goes to the position of player D

EXERCISE 36

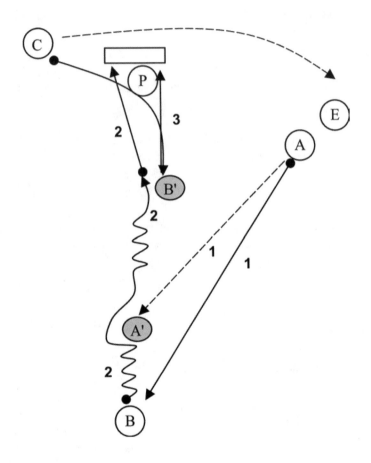

Technical objective

- ◆   SHOT AT GOAL
- ◆   LOW-GROUND PASS
- ◆   LOB PASS
- ◆   FEINT AND DRIBBLING THE BALL

Description

Four (or six) players are involved, with several balls.
This exercise must be carried out both clockwise and counterclockwise.
A and C have a ball.

1 -   A passes to B and runs to position A'

2 -   B receives, dribbles the ball toward A who tackles him in position A'; B beats A with a feint and shoots at goal

3 -   C makes a lob pass to B, who, on the volley, takes a second shot at goal from position B'

Next position

Player A goes to the position of player B
Player B goes to the position of player C
Player C goes to the position of player A

EXERCISE 37

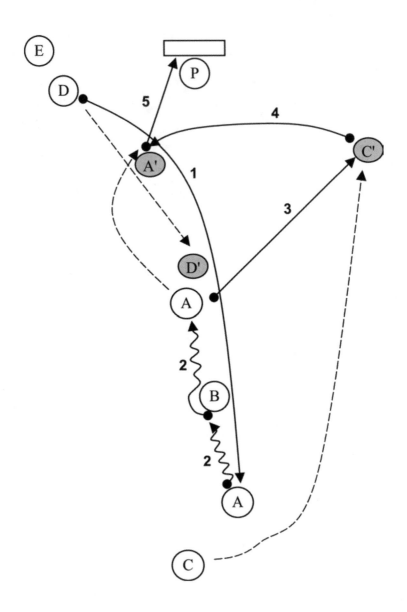

Technical objective

- SHOT AT GOAL
- PASS
- OVERLAPPING RUN
- DRIBBLING THE BALL
- FEINT AND DRIBBLING THE BALL

Description

Five (or six) players are involved, plus the goalkeeper.
This exercise must be carried out both clockwise and counterclockwise.
D has the ball.

1 - D makes a lob pass to A

2 - A receives, dribbles the ball toward B, and beats him with a feint, dribbling the ball past him

3 - A makes a pass to C, who carries out an overlapping run on the wing and receives in position C', while D tackles A in position D'

4 - C makes a cross-pass to A, who runs to position A' to receive

5 - A shoots at goal

Next position

Player A goes to the position of player C
Player C goes to the position of player D
Player B goes to the position of player A
Player D goes to the position of player B

EXERCISE 38

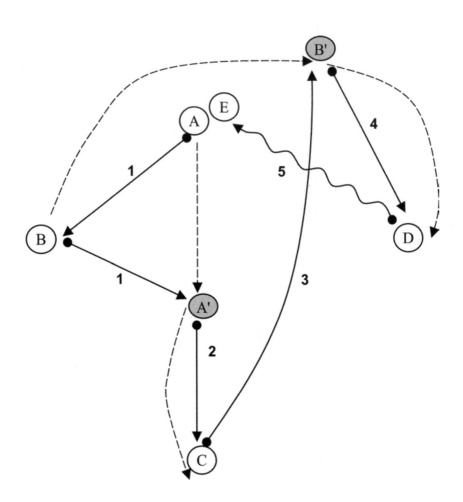

Technical objective

- LOW-GROUND PASS
- LOB PASS
- TRIANGULATION

Description

Five players are involved.
A has the ball.

1 - A carries out a triangulation with B and runs to position A' to receive the return pass

2 - A passes to C and follows the ball

3 - C makes a lob pass to B, who runs to receive in position B'

4 - B receives the ball, passes it to D and follows the ball

5 - D dribbles the ball toward player E, who restarts the exercise

Next position

Player A goes to the position of player C
Player B goes to the position of player D
Player C goes to the position of player B
Player D goes to the position of player A

EXERCISE 39

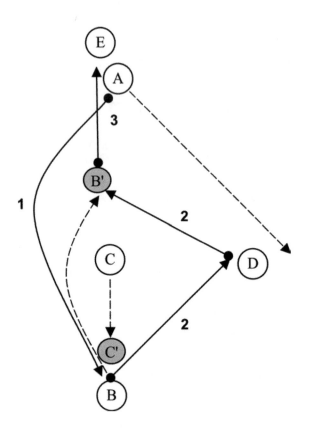

Technical objective
- LOW-GROUND PASS
- TRIANGULATION
- LOB PASS

Description
Five players are involved.
A has the ball.

1 - A makes a lob pass to B and goes to position D

2 - B makes a wall pass with D to beat the tackle from C in position C'

3 - B receives in position B', then passes to E who restarts the exercise

Next position
Player A goes to the position of player D
Player D goes to the position of player C
Player C goes to the position of player B
Player B goes to the position of player A

EXERCISE 40

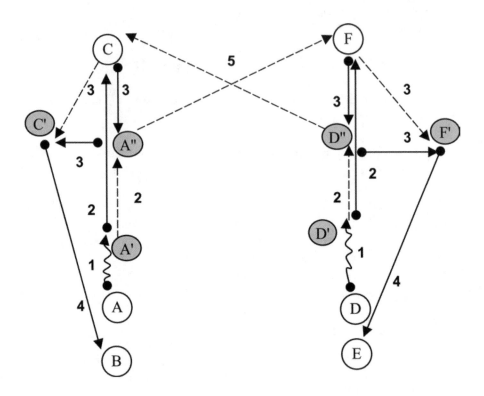

Technical objective

♦   DRIBBLING THE BALL

♦   PASS

♦   TRIANGULATION

Description

Two groups of three or more players are involved.

A and D have a ball.

1 -   A and D dribble the ball to positions A' and D' respectively

2 -   A and D make a low-ground pass to C and F respectively, and
follow the ball

3 -   C and F return the ball by a wall pass to A (in position A") and D
(in position D") respectively, and carry out a wall pass with them

4 -   C and F receive the return pass in position C' and F', and pass to
B and E, who restart the exercise

5 -   A and D make a diagonal run and take the place of players F and
C respectively

Next position

Player A goes to the position of player F

Player D goes to the position of player C

Player C goes to the position of player A

Player F goes to the position of player D

In-depth analysis I
MOTOR LEARNING

Motor learning is characterized by a **change of behavior.**
This means that, at the end of a coaching process, the player must be able to carry out, in a competitive situation, an activity which he was previously not able to carry out.
If this does not happen, then it means that **the motor skill has not been learned.**
If this occurs, the coach must **reconsider** either the method he used to coach, or the coaching plan.
Let us consider some important concepts which may be useful for understanding what "learning" means.
The brain's primary function is to receive sensorial stimuli, convert them into information and organize a proper cognitive or motor response (see In -depth analysis 1.1).
Among the various stimuli, the visual ones, which involve both a sensory aspect (sight) and a cognitive one (the perception of meaningful stimuli), give the brain the greatest amount of space-time information during the motor activity.
Therefore in sports, as in all other activities which involve the execution of dynamic actions, the **visual-perceptive-motor** cognitive mechanism is most important (see In-depth analysis 1.2).
Also, stimuli based on one's **own perception** are important: they reach the brain in a parallel way and integrate with the information coming from the perception of the outside world.
The movements made in a sport represent the end product of a series of phenomena that starts with a sensory perception and continues with a motor action which, continuously updated by the perceptive system, enables a person to carry out quick adjustments.
The athlete's perception of meaningful stimuli from the environment is a "learned" process; it is based on previous experience, and can therefore be improved by coaching, so as to enable a player to give a performance which is more and more appropriate to the characteristics of the sport he practices.

When the athlete is in a context that he sees (sensory function) and recognizes (cognitive function), he can give a response (motor function) which corresponds to the motor ability that he has already learned.
If the environment is "read" properly, this enables the athlete to face a

specific problem with a certain "continuity" (due to technical-tactical coaching), and if the athlete's osteo-myo-articular structures have been sufficiently adapted (due to physical-athletic training), then **the motor action is likely to be successful**.

If not, the motor action will not be correct and this will show that either the technical-tactical coaching or the physical-athletic training (or even both) is insufficient.

We can therefore say that the environment (that is, the exercises proposed in the coaching session) in which the athlete operates can stimulate the following responses:

- **Motor responses that are not suitable to the requirements of that sport**

  This situation corresponds to the initial stage of learning. The athlete cannot master his movements with continuity even in the coaching sessions, and does not make meaningful corrections.

- **Motor responses that are known, but have not been "learned"**

  This is the intermediate stage of learning. During the competition, the performance of the athlete is not constant and he makes many mistakes, while during the coaching session he shows that he is more and more able to correct his mistakes.

- **Motor responses that are automatic**

  This is the final stage of learning. During the competition, the athlete makes the correct movements with continuity.

A coach might also have the opportunity to coach a "talented" player; one characterized by strong personal motivation, a natural bent for learning, and the will to employ all the physical-athletic abilities which are necessary to execute, in the most effective possible way, what is being coached.

A young player who is considered **"talented"** is not necessarily one who demonstrates presently that he has the ability to play soccer at a high level. The term refers instead to a player who has the potential to learn to play soccer very well in the future, depending greatly on the content of the coaching and on the way the content is conveyed by the coach.

The talented young player can:

- employ his abilities in an adaptive way, according to the situations;
- learn new abilities very quickly;
- immediately and successfully make use of suggested corrections;
- combine his abilities according to changing situations;

- very quickly adapt his behavior to the various situations;
- easily synthesize complex variations of the motor program;
- modify, without difficulty, a highly automatic motor activity;
- control his speed of performance of a movement in response to the real requirements of a given situation;
- quickly integrate new elements with an already learned technique;
- easily solve problems that are difficult for others;
- complete his technical actions in an efficient and elegant way, with smooth and effective movements;
- repeat a motor activity several times, with both space-time and dynamic precision;
- improve those motor processes which are not completely profitable in order to obtain maximum quality results.

In-depth analysis 1.1
SENSORY RECEPTORS

Interpreting sensory stimuli and learning how to respond to them is one of the body's basic needs. This continuous interaction produces the adaptation process.

The contact with the outside world is made through specialized nerve structures, called "sensory receptors". However, we do not receive sensory information solely from the surrounding environment, but also from within our own body. The sensory systems that receive the signals from different origins can be divided into three groups:

- exteroceptive system;
- proprioceptive system;
- interoceptive system.

- The **exteroceptive system** is sensitive to stimuli coming from the surrounding environment; it includes the visual, auditory and touch systems.
- The **proprioceptive system** gives information on the position of one's own body and on the relationship of the body's position in space. Vestibular receptors belong to this system too. Due to its remarkable speed, the vestibular system contributes to the stabilization of the images in the retina during the movements of the head. In fact, while data processing by the retina is relatively slow, with a latency of about 70 milliseconds, the latency of the oculo-vestibular reflex is only 10 milliseconds and therefore can respond to dynamic situations more quickly.
- The **interoceptive system** gives the brain information on events within the body, for example, blood pressure, concentration of glucose in the blood, etc.

In the sports activity, the stimuli that determine the quality of the motor response are those that refer to the exteroceptive system (especially to the visual system) and to the proprioceptive system, as they regulate balance and give information on the condition of the muscles and of the joints.

♦ **Joint kinesthetic proprioceptors**

Proprioception includes the sense of balance and the sense of the position of the arms and legs. The sense of the position of the arms and legs includes those sensations that originate from stimulation of the mechanoreceptors and inform on the position and on the movement of the joints.

There are three kinds of peripheral mechanoreceptors:

- Most **mechanoreceptors of the joint capsules** are slow adaptation receptors that are stimulated by any joint movement. Only a small minority of joint receptors are quick adaptation receptors: these are the rare Pacinian corpuscles, located in the joints.

  Joint receptors are static and dynamic at the same time. They can be identified with the numerous Ruffini cylinders and with the Mazzoni's corpuscles, located in the joint ligaments.

  At the beginning of the movement, these receptors discharge at a very high rate and this allows assessment of the speed of the angular movement. When the movement stops, and the joint remains fixed in the new position, the discharge stabilizes at a lower rate and this gives information on the angle formed by the joint.

- Like joint receptors, **Skin mechanoreceptors** do not determine an accurate assessment of the leg or arm position or movement, therefore they are used by the nervous system only in part.

- As for the **muscle mechanoreceptors**, the assessment of the angle of the joint is made on the basis of the information related to the length of the muscle, which is given by the receptors of the neuromuscular spindle, a structure which is stimulated by stretching and acts automatically, activating the contraction reflex of the muscle itself.

Therefore, the main function of the joint receptors seems to be one of signaling the position of an arm or leg when it is in extreme conditions of flexing or stretching, while the information on the movement, and so on the length of the muscles, is given by the spindle receptors.

Both types of information can reach the player's consciousness, enabling him to control his movements.

Control based on proprioception, though, is not commonly observed among young players, as they lack the necessary experience to know how to "listen to" their body.

It is particularly difficult to "feel" the position (inclination, flexion, rotation, etc.) of one's own body parts, especially during the performance of a complex motor action such as a technical soccer exercise.

This is why we think that those corrections suggested by the coach that use only this way of motor control are not correct, and must instead be integrated with corrections that stimulate the visual- perceptive way.

However, in the first phase of motor learning, corrections that rely on proprioception are useful, since they integrate all the information from outside, so that when the athlete makes movements that are so incorrect that they might jeopardize his ability to develop further and more complex learning, they may be corrected.

In-depth analysis 1.2
VISUAL PERCEPTION

Visual perception enables an individual to get more and better information on the world around him than he can from any other sense. Given the same period of time, no other type of sensory perception can give the same amount of information to an individual as rapidly.

Movement is something closely linked with visual perception.

The human being has developed a considerable degree of independence in the control of the movements of the head and of the eyes. The combination of the movements of the head and of the eyes, explained by precise neuro-physiological mechanisms, enables man to maintain a certain stability in visual perception even in conditions of high dynamism, changes of posture and sudden movements of the head.

Visual information guides the motor system; however, the visual system alone would be insufficient without the involvement and integration of the other sensory systems, especially the vestibular and proprioceptive systems. The ability to execute perfect motor control depends on some functions of the nervous system, which largely controls movements without the individual's conscious awareness.

There are parts of the body of which the individual is aware and to which he can send orders or from which he can receive sensations. There are also parts of the body which almost seem to be "unknown" to the individual, and are therefore more difficult to consciously control.

Many muscles are used in a completely automatic way, and so it is often impossible for an individual to realize whether or not a movement is correct.

However, the muscles do not only receive orders from the brain before the action, but they also exchange messages during the movement via a feedback circuit, integrating the messages with data coming in real time from vestibular, proprioceptive and visual canals.

Especially in the first phase of technical learning, the coaching method must make the most of these considerations.

Every sport requires different physical and visual abilities. In particular, it is visual abilities which influence the accomplishment of objectives. The visual process controls the physical and functional performance that an athlete can express. In fact, about 80% of motor functions are executed based on visual perception. Therefore, if an athlete has a poor visual system, his physical abilities will be adversely affected.

Visual perception represents a subjective and impromptu interpretation of stimuli which after being received are processed and compared with the information stored in the individual's memory. This is why we cannot consider visual perception only as the product of information received by the eyes; it is a complex phenomenon which largely depends on the individual's mental qualities.

An athlete does not perceive all that he watches; he perceives more easily those stimuli that he "expects" to see.

A mistake in the athlete's movement, based on his incorrect analysis of the environment, is often due to the fact that the athlete does not know what to look for, or cannot recognize some environmental aspects as elements that could help him.

For this purpose, the technical and tactical exercises in the coaching sessions should always be oriented toward making young players develop specific experience and knowledge, using a large variety of situations/problems mostly taken from soccer.

Motor learning is largely based on visual perception. The adaptation process takes place based on a continuous sensory feedback, through which every part of the body "communicates" with the brain, sending and receiving information.

The result of motor responses depends on the precision of the sensory feedback. Visual perception generates a feedback toward itself and toward the other sensory processes, generating a further feedback which assesses the correctness and the effectiveness of the action executed, which will then be modified and improved.

The feedback generated by the proprioceptive and visual systems plays two important roles in the control of the movement. It guides the trajectory of the body, including the legs and the arms, and it also provides for fine adjustments, in order to complete the action.

The perception of the movement is the end product of a chain of phenomena which characterize its speed, coordination and precision, and which are an indication of the way in which the body functions.

Physical condition, sensory processes and mental processes are three aspects which determine one single phenomenon: the individual's overall performance. Considering them separately means dealing with the athlete's performance in a limited way and reducing the athlete's actual capacity for improvement.

As we have already said, at brain level, every bit of information which is perceived is compared with a kind of data bank which is continuously updated and represents the individual's unique experience.

The event which is currently being perceived may be more or less correlated with the individual's past experience. This correlation determines the meaning of what the individual perceives. This has a considerable influence on his action; in fact, the time necessary to process a stimulus is time that is not available for the execution of a quick and accurate response. This happens also during the analysis of the movement of objects in surrounding space. The irregular bounce of the ball on the ground is an example of a situation where it sometimes is difficult to be ready to react. Being caught by surprise, and as a consequence, not being able to react properly, is the result of a perceptive and motor experience which is unsuitable for facing a particular situation.

Getting ready for a certain event is an extremely important parameter, which influences both speed and precision of the response, so as to accomplish a perfect integration between data from outside and data from inside one's body.

However, even in the presence of precise and quick perceptive processes, the result of the action may be inferior to the expected level if the physical condition of the athlete is not suitable to the movements he is expected to make. Likewise, poor performance may occur when, although the physical condition is optimum, the perceptive processes are not sufficiently precise, quick and integrated.

We are aware that a coach's task, especially at a youth level, is to correct the mistakes made by the athlete.

However, we feel that it is necessary to point out the objective difficulty that an athlete has in certain situations, so that the coach can find the motor solutions which are suitable for reaching the coaching objective.

Let us consider a common event in soccer: the player is trying to steal the ball.

The perception of the movement of his own body and of an object outside it is the result of the integration between two important phenomena:

- the optimum condition of his body, both from the physiologic and perceptive point of view;
- the physical characteristics of the object that moves across space.

The variations in these phenomena involve, first of all, the fact that no two athletes perceive their movements and the movement of the objects around them in the same way. The motor reaction urged by outside stimuli is extremely personal; suffice it to say that, in addition to the millions of stimuli coming to the brain from the retina, the brain must also process information that takes into account the posture of the body, the inclination of the head, the condition of balance, etc.

For this purpose, the brain establishes some priorities. For example, if the athlete is playing on a slippery field and has difficulty in keeping his balance, the brain will take into greater consideration vestibular and proprioceptive information, rather than visual information. The same thing happens when an athlete is about to intercept the ball while he is being tackled by an opponent in physical contact with him. Here too, the brain will give priority to the condition of balance, rather than to the analysis of the trajectory of the ball, with an increase of the possibility of error of movement.

Since every perceptive phenomenon is compared with the player's past experience in real time, it is important to "stock" enough experience in the player by coaching the players with pre-situation and situation exercises, in order to get them accustomed to facing situations and problems that they are likely to experience during a match.

In-depth analysis 2
COGNITIVE PROCESSES

The development of the cognitive abilities (motivation, attention, perception, memory) that provide for learning improvement, is closely connected to the way in which the coach organizes and directs the exercises during a coaching session. Of course, in the development of a learning process, these mental mechanisms overlap and contribute simultaneously to the learning. We are going to deal with them separately only for the purpose of discussing their meaning.

Motivation
One of the most important objectives of coaching is to motivate the athlete toward ever better performances.
In soccer, we can define **motivation** as the "willingness to accomplish certain objectives", which vary according to the age of the athletes. Often, in order to reach them, the athletes will have to overcome difficulty and make sacrifices.
The athlete's motivation is shown by the way he faces the task he has been given, by the level he reaches in the pre-established objectives, and by his perseverance in his attempts at achieving the objectives.
A strong motivation gives a considerable boost to the improvement of the **quality of learning** (learning is easier and more detailed).
Talking about motivation, we think it is reductionistic to say that the exercises must be, above all, entertaining; in fact, even though the playful aspect should not be underestimated, it must not be the only point of reference. We think that the exercises must have such characteristics as to stimulate in the young player a **"natural interest"** in what he does; this is what psychology calls "primary motivation". In addition, we should not forget that a young player may find **"important"** what is important for his coach. Psychology, which calls this phenomenon "secondary motivation", considers it a positive factor in the motivation to learning.
The coach has an important role in motivation, too.

The coach must stimulate the player's enthusiasm
Soccer has the advantage that, at least at a youth level, the player's motivation is very strong.
The task of the coach is to keep this asset alive, through activities that stimulate the young player's will to continuously improve his skills.
In order to be motivating, the exercises aimed at improving a movement

or a tactical element **must fulfill** the young player's expectations ("I enjoy doing these exercises, because I realize I am learning") and he **must like** them; for this purpose, they should be organized in an interesting way and with variations (the objectives should be pursued through the application of numerous variables).

The coach must stimulate the player's self-motivation

The next objective is to maintain the player's level of motivation.

We think that, to accomplish this objective, the coach should explain the purpose of each of the exercises that he employs in the coaching session. In fact, the athlete needs to know the importance of the means the coach uses, as they pertain to the development and the improvement of the player's performance.

For this purpose, we suggest that in a brief talk with the players before the coaching session, the coach should explain and **emphasize the main theme** that will be coached on the field.

In addition, since the players must always know what the coach expects of them, he should repeat the same kind of brief talk before every exercise, emphasizing the aspect to which he wants the players to pay special attention.

In other words, the coach must be able to characterize the coaching session with a **"general theme"**, and each exercise with a **"specific theme"** which, for the purpose of developing the player's learning process, becomes the object of particular **attention** and necessary **corrections**.

At the end of the session, the coach must **reinforce the player's memory** of what has been done and said during the session, pointing out with a brief talk both the positive and negative results that he has observed. With regard to the negative results, the coach should suggest the solutions which could have been employed and then deal in the next session with the problems he observed in the previous coaching session.

The coach must clearly define both the objectives and the most appropriate plan to achieve them

If the athlete knows the coach's objective, he can mentally anticipate what performance he has to execute and what results he has to achieve.

This strongly influences the athlete's action, since:

- **The objective affects motivation**

  The athlete carries out all the actions that he believes will accomplish what he understands to be the coach's objectives.

- **The objective directs the motor activity**
The athlete's movements are organized and controlled to accomplish the coach's objective.
- **The objective controls the motor activity**
When he knows what he wants to accomplish, the athlete controls the relation between his intentions and the results obtained.

If the coach wants the exercises to be successful for purposes of achieving the objective, they must:
- **be clearly formulated**
Especially with young players, the coach's explanation of the exercise must be made using words with which the players are familiar, and must be summarized at crucial points to help the young player remember. Additional elements can be explained during the performance of the exercise or while the coach is correcting the players' performance.
- **be challenging**
The objectives must always be a challenge for the players. Objectives that are easily reached, or that cannot be reached, do not succeed in motivating the players.
- **be explained**
The athlete must know the relevance, in terms of their benefit to the player as well as to the team, of executing activities prescribed by the coach.

Once he has established the objectives, the coach should ask himself what obstacles could possibly prevent their accomplishment. This involves a thorough analysis of the players' characteristics, taking into account their skills, their ability to learn and the physical-athletic qualities that they can express.

Attention

Attention is the mental mechanism through which an individual can select an "object" from those contained in his environment, in order to accurately analyze it so that it becomes a part of his knowledge.
Attention is an intermediate process between motivation and perception. Therefore, if an exercise stimulates strong interest in the athlete, he will pay more attention and will be ready to understand.
Attention requires an individual's mental resources, especially in the initial phases of any learning process. This is why the athlete at first seems tech-

nically awkward or unable to satisfactorily carry out tactical actions. The explanation commonly given by coaches for this inability is that the athlete "does not reason". Actually, it is the other way round; the athlete employs too much psychic energy either on technical details which are not yet completely automatic, or attempting to solve tactical aspects which are often irrelevant to the achievement of the objective.

Developing **conscious control** over one's own movements (technical competence) or in the play environment (ball, field, teammates, opponents) is a "slow" process which cannot be positively applied during competitive activity.

Paying attention, and thus slowing down one's motor response, is the price each individual player has to pay. At the same time, it is a necessary prerequisite for starting any learning process which, after becoming automatic through continuous practice, will enable the player to optimize his sports achievements.

The experience acquired during the practice session enables the player to act with an ever increasing automatic control and with an ever diminishing conscious control, requiring a reduced amount of attention and achieving the possibility of playing with better overall performance.

"Seeing and doing" without too many conscious interventions is the final objective for the coach, who knows that as long as this remains to be accomplished, he should be prepared to expect a high percentage of mistakes from his players.

More experienced players have the characteristic of displaying more effective ways of processing information than do younger players. In fact, as they have more motor responses which have already become automatic due to years of practice, they can dedicate more attention to those situational variations inherent in soccer, which they can consciously influence.

With younger players, coaches should propose exercises that can stimulate the player's ability to selectively apply a **wide or narrow focus**, as well as the ability to switch from one kind of focus to the other.

In this book, the exercises that we recommend for the first phase of learning are intended to pursue the above said objectives. In fact, the exercises that we propose alternately stimulate both attention focused on the stimuli coming from one's own body and attention focused on the control of the result of the technical activity which the athlete has used to participate, for example, in a tactical action.

Let us investigate this, by dealing with what we call **dispensed attention**. As in all other sports, in soccer the athlete continuously faces situations that involve individual, group and team technical and tactical skills.

This means that, for the entire match, a player has to perform two tasks: one technical and the other tactical. If the tasks are easy, his action is successful. However, sometimes the two tasks interfere with each other.

In order to explain the results obtained from **double tasks**, it is necessary to assume that the resources of **attention-concentration** are strictly limited.

The quality of the performance of two simultaneous tasks depends on how much concentration each task requires.

If the concentration required by the two tasks does not exceed the total amount of available resources of concentration, then the quality of the performance is good. On the other hand, when the resources are not enough to meet the demands of the two tasks, then the performance is poor.

One key phenomenon that determines an evident improvement in the performance of double tasks is the **practical execution** of the exercises. The movements become automatic in the following ways:

- Whenever a stimulus is met and processed, specific mnestic traces are stored.
- Practicing with a certain kind of stimulus leads to recognition of more and more information about the stimulus itself, thus learning what to do with it.
- As knowledge increases, during the activity there is quick recall from memory of relevant information as soon as the proper stimulus is felt.

Motor performance becomes automatic when it is determined by immediate and direct recall of the memory of past solutions.

Finally, those processes which have become automatic result in excellent sports performances, since they:

- are fast;
- do not require attention, and so do not reduce the ability to perform other tasks;
- are not conscious;
- always occur when the appropriate stimulus is felt.

Perception

Perception is the expression of an activity that integrates several complex functions which are used to recognize outside reality.

In general, there are two main sources of information that can be used to properly perceive the outside world. One is sensory input, and the other is the memory of past experiences.

Accordingly, "perception" implies processes like the formulation of hypotheses and expectations, in order to give a meaning to the information gathered by sensory organs.

Therefore, the formulation both of incorrect hypotheses and of wrong expectations, as well as the absence of hypotheses and expectations, leads to mistakes in perception.

What is the relationship between sensory perception and motor activity? Sensory perception is directly correlated to motor performance.

Unsatisfactory motor coordination (the presence of mistakes) is **in direct proportion** to unsatisfactory sensory perception. This demonstrates that pre-arranged motor programs do not exist, and therefore there is no absolute memory from which information can be drawn. Instead, there are nervous processes that, influenced by muscle feedback and by continuous incoming information, run the movements in real time. If there is no information, **the movement fails**.

Situational exercises are very important because they enable the athlete to have meaningful perceptive experiences and to employ in the play the corresponding movements.

Sensory perception and motor coordination are undetectable to any introspection.

While what **is perceived** cannot be organized by reasoning, **perceptive analysis** can be made by using cortical functions. For example, the form of an object is perceived automatically and without intention, and the object is recognized by giving it a name or a meaning by a brain activity that refers to consciousness.

Therefore:

> - the athlete perceives some aspects of the environment that can be more or less meaningful, and the motor response that he gives depends on this perception;
> - the proof that a learning process has been carried out is in the fact that the athlete has practically demonstrated it. When a mistake occurs, then, even though the athlete carries out a control in order to correct himself, he will nevertheless be unable to influence, strictly speaking, the movements that he makes between one control and the next.

A young player needs many exercises and many years of practice before he can develop sufficient knowledge of the variety of situations he is apt to experience in a game, so that he can carry out fewer and fewer controls and thereby execute his movements more effectively during the game.

The practical exercises to employ must be targeted to support the player's and his teammates' abilities, in such areas as perception of space, time, pace, speed of movement of the ball, etc. These are qualities that the young player will develop only by exercises that employ specific situations of play.

Memory

Sports performance depends also on the player's capacity to remember information for a given period of time, so that it can be used whenever it is necessary.

Although memory capacity is a cognitive aspect which has not yet been investigated deeply, some studies have shown that experienced players are better than young and inexperienced players at temporarily remembering useful information.

The prevailing thinking is that this capacity cannot be generalized for every mnemonic task, but is limited to memorization of such information as is typical in the context of the athlete's sport. This is probably made easier by a wide associative network of specific knowledge acquired through constant practice.

We should not forget that, in order to learn a new movement, it is necessary to practice it correctly and for a long time. In addition, learning is easier if teaching is connected with an intense and positive emotional situation. In fact, the quality and the amount of information that can be stored in one's memory can be increased considerably in various ways; for example, by organizing exercises which are characterized by strong **emotional sensations** (such as competition among the players or between groups), and, above all, by having the players perform the proposed activity repeatedly, **within a short period of time**.

In fact, from the point of view of "method", if a player does not do the exercises correctly he must immediately have the opportunity to try again, using the new information he has been given.

In this way, the player is less likely to be negatively distracted by the environment (including by his teammates, other technical or tactical tasks, etc.). Finally, work in small groups determines the most suitable conditions for memorizing technical-tactical themes, since the cycle of the organization of the exercise (try-correction-try) is short.

From the practical point of view, the best performance can be obtained when the subsequent try is proposed while the athlete is still concentrating on the result he obtained in the previous try.

In-depth analysis 3
TIMING

In order to understand the importance of "timing", we should first consider the concept of "technical movements".

The correct and practical execution of a technical movement involves optimum employment of physical and psycho-emotional energies, as well as specific motor control of the movement being executed. Therefore, technical movements cannot be considered only as solutions to a coordination problem; they must be considered as the result of the integration of all the constituents that determine performance, that is, coordination, physical and emotional skills, as well as tactics.

The player's ability to respond with the appropriate motor activity is determined not only by how much and what information he receives from the surrounding environment, but also by the point in time in which he processes this information.

The visual system is man's best time machine, and for this reason, especially in sports, greater expression of physical power cannot compensate for incorrect or insufficient information processing with respect to **"timing"**.

Performance is often below optimum level not because the player executes an inappropriate technical movement, but because he executes it at the wrong time.

Timing and the ability to quickly visualize an event in order to be ready for it before it occurs, are the keys to achieving optimum results.

Success in sport often depends on the "space-time precision" that comes from the application of the proper measure of strength. In one of our previous books , we showed the extreme importance of the inseparable combination of "quality" (form of the movement) and "intensity" (space-time relationship) in both physical-athletic and technical-tactical coaching work loads.

"Timing" is an extremely interesting ability, and epitomizes the most typical expression of talent in young players: the ability to be at the right place at the right time, controlling in an optimum way the supply of muscle energy, the speed of performance and the form of the movement.

The success of the technical movement is defined by space-time precision, combined with "quickness" as that is expressed with the player's application of the proper measure of strength, that is, the variable application of strength, depending on the cadenced sequence (coordination) which is demanded at different times during the match (endurance).

Timing, as a general ability, is the result of a long process during which the individual must be coached in the most complete possible way.

Since every phase of learning soccer skills abounds with mistakes and inaccuracies, it is only through a method based on **acting-correcting-acting** that the coach can teach the players to carry out a more successful action.

In addition, the number of corrections made by the coach and the precision with which he makes them, determine whether or not the final result is correct. Often, an ill-timed correction by the coach can induce the player to make a correct movement at the wrong time, or an incorrect movement at the right time, thus frustrating the achievement of the objective of the practice session.

In-depth analysis 4
INTENTIONALITY

Intentionality is the mental aspect that precedes the beginning of every voluntary motor act.

The time between the moment an intention arises and its transformation into action is variable and depends on several factors, ranging from the difficulty in making the movement, to the interferences determined by the environment, to the subject's ability to face a known or previously unknown new situation, etc.

The objective of coaching is to shorten the length of time required between the mental act and the expression of the practical activity. During the learning process, "the intention of..." must be very clear in the player's mind, since it corresponds to the kind of movement he has to execute. It is only after executing the pre-established movement that the athlete realizes the difference between what he wanted to execute and what he has executed.

Coaching must result in the athlete's visual-perceptive-motor system stimulating in him the so-called **intention-reaction** phenomenon, which enables him to integrate with the environment in response to the requirements of the actual competition.

In a team sport, in order to execute any tactical intention on the basis of what he perceives, the player must solve three important problems:

  - **Where to act?**
  - **When to act?**
  - **How to act?**

In order to better understand the concepts of "where", "when" and "how", let us consider an example with an action that requires excellent analysis and action capacities: intercepting the ball on defense.

With the term **"intercepting the ball on defense"**, we refer to stealing the ball, taking it away from the opponent who was supposed to have received it.

First of all, interception presupposes that a player can "hide" his intention, for the purpose of taking his opponent by surprise.

The answer to the question **"where** to intercept the ball?" is "in the free space", that is, on the possible path that connects the opponent who passes the ball with the one who is about to receive it.

If the path is short, that is, if the two opponents are close to each other, then the ball is difficult to intercept. If the path is medium-distance or long, then, since the two opponents are quite far from each other, interception is easier. In this case, the player must try to intercept the ball in the part of the path which is closer to the opponent who is supposed to receive it.

Having a tactical intention means that **"the idea of intercepting"** must be present in all the team's players, in every part of the field, starting from the moment when the team loses possession. By definition, then, this means that this intention must also be present during the defensive back movement, which must be active.

In order to try to **intercept the ball**, the player must anticipate the direction and the path of the ball. In order to do that, he must orient his body in such a way as to have, within his field of vision, both the opponent with the ball and the one who is the possible receiver.

Possible mistakes in particular moments of play

- If the player **focuses only on the ball and on the opponent with the ball,** he is not in a position to control the opponent who may be preparing to receive it, thus allowing this opponent to place himself in the correct position to receive the ball (unmarking movement).
- If the player **focuses only on the opponent who may be preparing to receive the ball,** it means that he is not watching the ball and thus may be taken by surprise when the ball gets near him and he may not be able to react properly.

For purposes of controlling the opponent with the ball and the possible receiver, it is not enough to simply concentrate on the proper orientation of the body. It is also necessary that the player learn to alternate the gathering of information from these two elements (the opponent with the ball and the possible receiver), by moving and turning the head, so that he can visualize the possible path of the ball at any moment.

The answer to the question **"when** to intercept the ball?" is "At the right time".

Since he is aware that interception is possible starting from the moment the ball is kicked (as its path cannot be changed after that), the defending player, while controlling the opposing possible receiver, must at the same time observe the behavior of the opponent with the ball and look for meaningful information from him.

This fundamental consideration determines the time of the action.

The timing of the action also depends on the distance between the defender and the possible path of the ball, since:

- if the defender acts too soon, or too close to the opponent with the ball, interception is less likely to happen (unless the opponent who makes the pass makes a mistake) since the opponent, seeing the defender's action or position, may change his mind and not pass.

- if the defender is too far from the opponent who is supposed to receive the ball, then interception is again very unlikely. After the pass is made and received, the defender must run after the opponent who now has the ball, and therefore is unable to control him.

There is then another problem which is closely related to the previous one. Depending on the score of the game at the time (whether one's team is winning or losing) and on the opponent's abilities, there are some times during the game which are more suitable than others for purposes of intercepting the ball. The ability to assess the difference between the two teams will determine whether or not to apply this tactical intention.

The answer to the question "**how** to intercept the ball?" is "In the best way possible, so that the intercepting player can keep possession". Specific soccer skills play a decisive role at this point.

Let us consider now how the process of integration between "intention" and "action" is stimulated in the phase of technical learning and improvement.

Motor program

An important element of this process of integration involves the nervous system's selection of the proper **"motor program"**. This process can be illustrated by considering, for example, that before the player makes a movement with the leg to kick the ball, his nervous system selects that motor program which specifies both the sequence of muscle activation which is necessary to bring the foot to the desired point and also the extent of contraction of the various muscles.

The main constituents of this motor program are developed by three cortical regions of the brain:

- **the supplementary motor area,**
- **the pre-motor cortex,**
- **the back parietal cortex.**

Together, these three regions of the brain determine the individual movements which are necessary to result in a single proper action.

The supplementary motor area

The clearest demonstration of the role played by the supplementary motor area in programming the sequences of complex individual movements has recently been given by studies on cerebral blood flow in selected cortical regions.

This method is based on the fact that local blood flow increases as the neuronal activity increases.

Based on this significant finding, it has been possible to verify that, when the subjects were asked to repeat a certain sequence of movements only mentally, without actually executing them, an increase in the blood flow was observed. There was an increase in the activity of the neurons in the supplementary motor area, without any concurrent activity increase in the motor cortex. This fact shows that the supplementary motor area is involved in programming motor sequences.

Pre-motor cortex

It has been assumed that the primary role of the pre-motor cortex is to control proximal and axial muscles, and that the pre-motor cortex needs to be activated, in the initial phases of a movement, in order to determine the general orientation of the body.

Recent studies have demonstrated that the neurons of the pre-motor cortex respond to sensory stimuli in a way that is consistent with the subject's **"intention"** to use the information to guide the movement. Therefore, when we move an arm toward a target, some neurons of the pre-motor cortex are immediately activated as soon as the stimulus is perceived, while other neurons respond only when the movement is actually made.

In experiments, it has been observed that a specific class of neurons becomes active in the interval between the introduction of the first stimulus (intention) and the introduction of the signal of the beginning of the movement. These neurons seem to encode the instruction that they have received, since their activity changes in relation to what must be done when the signal of the beginning of the movement is introduced.

The back parietal cortex

The back parietal cortex is extremely important, since it gives the necessary space information to execute movements toward an object.

Clinical and experimental data show that the back parietal lobe plays a vital role in processing the sensory signals that guide voluntary movements.

Two classes of neurons are particularly significant, as they can play a role in the process involved in beginning a movement.

The first class includes the so-called **projection neurons**, which are activated only when an arm or leg moves toward a nearby object.

These neurons do not respond to any form of passive sensory stimulus and, if the object that had aroused interest is no longer there, they are not activated when the arm or leg is moved toward the same space where the object was previously.

The second class of neurons, called **contact neurons**, becomes active when the arm or leg gets close to the object that arouses interest.

Then, in the back parietal cortex there are some neurons that are activated by sensory stimuli, but only in a context of extremely specific behavioral motor responses.

In-depth analysis 5
INDIVIDUAL TACTICAL BEHAVIOR

Relationship between technical skills, individual tactical behavior and team tactical behavior (R. Capanna)

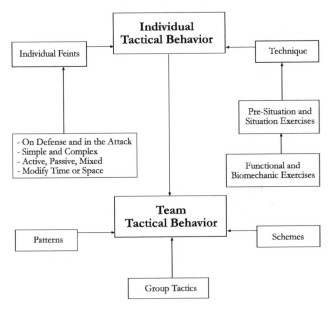

"Individual tactics" can be defined as "all those movements that, considering the actual situation, generate conditions that can be used to one's own advantage".

Therefore, individual tactical behavior can be considered as a short-term **action plan** that the coach must **always stimulate** whenever he teaches a new technical element. Especially with young players, the individual tactical behavior is expressed in different ways, depending on the player's:

- morphologic characteristics,
- physical-athletic capacities,
- technical skills and the way in which they have been acquired,
- level of perception ability, and the level of analysis and understanding of play situations,
- ability to control emotions.

In the player's mind there has to be the will to put the opponents in difficult conditions, even before he starts his motor action. This mental attitude comes from experience and coaching, therefore the coach must organize the exercises in such a way as to accomplish this objective.

The application of an individual tactical attitude presupposes having developed the following skills:

- **Individual tactics without the ball**

  For example:
  - applying various kinds of feints (see In-depth analysis 5.1);
  - changes of direction when facing an opponent;
  - proper alignment with respect to one's own goal and the opponent, in "man-marking" and "zone-marking" play;
  - overlapping, or cutting in, at the right moment and in the right place, etc.

- **Individual tactics with the ball**

  For example:
  - dribbling the ball;
  - defending the ball from an opponent;
  - making a feint, while making a pass, to put one's own marker in difficulty;
  - making a feint, while shooting at goal, so that the opposing goalkeeper does not immediately understand the shooter's intentions, etc.

As we have said above, individual feints must be coached and required during all the exercises, as they correspond to basic motor knowledge that enables the team to execute optimum team movements (team feints). Team feints imply the ability to apply a defensive and an offensive tactic.

The coach is responsible also for the **quality** of tactical coaching. His task is difficult and complex, and must be oriented toward optimization of the results through activities that employ patterns and schemes of play.
As the players' technical skills influence the team's tactical performance, such skills must be coached together with tactical elements, using situational exercises.
The following are some individual tactical intentions with which the players must be familiar on defense as well as in the attack.

Tactical intentions on defense

- **Play on the path of the ball in order to:**

- dissuade the opponent with the ball from passing it;
- intercept the ball.

♦ **Play on the opponent with the ball in order to:**
- hinder him;
- control him from within a certain distance.

Tactical intentions in the attack

♦ **Cooperate with the teammate with the ball in order to:**
- vacate space for the teammate;
- unmark oneself and receive a pass;
- receive the ball and shoot.

♦ **When one has the ball, the intention is to:**
- pass (cooperation with a teammate);
- face an opponent (1 on 1);
- shoot.

In-depth analysis 5.1
THE FEINT

Soccer is a sport in which performance depends on the interaction between environmental stimuli which vary continuously. The athlete's brain carries out important work to adapt to situations and use them to his own advantage. This may happen when two opponents face each other, each trying to frustrate the other's information processing system.

The feint can be defined as "an intentional attempt at deceiving the opponent in order to acquire an advantage in the competitive context".

Therefore, the feint can be considered as the basic unit for acquiring **tactical and strategic advantages** over the opponent (see In-depth analysis 5.1.1).

The kinds of feints

Feint on defense

Its objective is to make the opposing forward erroneously believe that the defender has made a mistake, which then leads the opposing forward to think he can exploit this "mistake" to his own advantage.

Feint in the attack

Its objective is to make the opposing defender erroneously believe that, in a particular zone of the field, the defender can start an action which could turn out to be very profitable for the defender.

Simple feint

It stimulates the opponent to "read" a fake signal.

Complex feint

It hinders the opponent's "reading" of a signal which, if read accurately, could be useful to him.

Active feint

The player who makes it has an active role, as he induces in the opponent an initial movement, which prevents the latter from reacting to the next action.

Passive feint

It creates in the opponent uncertainty about the player's real intentions.

The player must wait for the opponent to take the initiative, and then react accordingly.

The feint that modifies the time of play

It gives the player who makes it an advantage by enabling him to make a change of pace or speed.

The feint that modifies the space

It is the feint made by a player when he faces an opponent who is dribbling the ball, or, while with the ball, the movement he makes when he changes his direction while running in order to break free from marking.

The young players' will to make feints cannot often be actually effected, as they do not have the necessary technical abilities, or, better, because their attention during the play is more focused on the control of the technical movement than on the result determined by the execution of the feint. With the development of tactical coaching, the coach will try to teach his players to force their opponents "to react rather than act".

The more a player can build a situation which is highly predictable for himself while creating time pressure and mental fatigue in the opponent, the more likely he and his team will accomplish their individual and team positive objectives.

Of course, the feint should not be applied if there is too great a difference between the two teams from either the physical or technical point of view, or if, from the tactical point of view, the opponent is not able, for either lack of experience or ability, to read the action that implies a team feint.

In-depth analysis 5.1.1
TACTICS AND STRATEGY

With the term **"tactics"** we refer to a series of individual and team movements that, taking into account what really happens during the match, determine conditions that can be immediately exploited to one's own advantage.

On the other hand, with the term **"strategy"** we refer to the individual or team plan of attitude which is established before the match and is maintained during the match, taking into consideration both one's own, and the opponents', strong and weak points. As a consequence, strategy determines a mental planning which the athlete makes before the competition, trying to predict the opponents' possible decisions, without being able to influence them.

Therefore, "tactics" and "strategy" refer to a level which is higher than "motor action regulation": the psychic-intellectual level. Since tactical and strategic intentions come into play before the young player starts any motor activity, it means that they refer to the mental level and correspond to the persistent desire to prevail over the opponent.

The coach is responsible for stimulating this attitude in his players; the **tactical and strategic idea** from which this attitude derives must be improved and optimized through regular coaching, according to the players' physical abilities.

In-depth analysis 6
GROUP TACTICS

We use the term **"group tactics"** when forms of interaction among players of one or more sections of the team are carried out.
In the non-possession phase, group tactics is carried out:
- by applying pressure and by feinting pressure;
- by applying the concept of covering the marking teammate and the concept of "wait" when marking, etc.

In the possession phase, group tactics is carried out:
- by cooperating with one or more teammates of the defense and attack sections;
- by applying the concept of moving to support the teammate with the ball;
- by applying play schemes, etc.

Coaching note
We recommend the following exercises, which may be helpful for establishing an optimum cooperative relationship among teammates.
Alternate:
- cooperative activities in which the player with the ball causes the teammate who must receive "to move";
- cooperative activities in which the player without the ball makes himself available for the pass from the teammate with the ball.

We recommend the following exercises to accomplish the above objective:
- in uneven numbers: 2 on 1; 3 on 2; 4 on 3; 4 on 2; etc.
- in even numbers: 2 on 2; 3 on 3; 4 on 4; etc.
(applying overlappings and cut-ins)

In-depth analysis 7
TEAM TACTICS

We use the term **"team tactics"** to refer to the rational interaction among all the players of the team having the purpose of accomplishing a given objective.

Team tactics is carried out:

> - by getting the players to know the main patterns of play ("4-4-2"; "5-3-2"; "3-5-2"; etc.);
> - by applying offensive and defensive schemes of play.

The particular level of a team's tactical proficiency determines that team's possibilities of handling the match in different ways.

Let us consider how the tactical potential of a team can be identified.

- The team can apply simple tactical movements, and, if so, these movements will presumably be **familiar** to the opponents. This is an elementary level of play.

  Tactical cooperation is prescribed, and does not depend on those solutions that develop during the match, in response to the actual events which take place, and so, this form of tactical cooperation takes place without any analysis of the visual information coming from the play environment. The tactical exercise is organized according to prescribed theoretical models given by the coach, who tries to anticipate, often mistakenly, the possible solutions that the opponents may apply during the match.

- During the match, the team can apply **unexpected** cooperation due to the ability of some players to find alternative solutions which have not been prescribed by the coach. Even though this ability may be thought to depend on the athlete's "innate" talent, it is greatly influenced by the way in which the coach organizes the practice sessions. In fact, it is easier for the athlete to give way to his inventiveness during the match, where the coach, even though maintaining a common pre-established idea of tactical cooperation, supports and motivates inventiveness and initiative among his players.

- The team presents **predictable** solutions.
  This means that the action is "empty" from the point of view of individual and/or group tactics. In this case, the players make movements that can easily be read by the opponent.

- The team can present **unpredictable** actions.
  Some players are tactically effective and able to cooperate while "hiding" their real intentions.
  This situation gives the whole team a considerable advantage.

From the above considerations, it can be inferred that, in the competitive phase, every team can perform according to one of the following three levels:

Level 1

The team presents a **familiar and predictable** tactical activity.
We can therefore assume that the team's competitive performance is poor.

Level 2

The team presents a tactical activity which is **familiar** to the opponents, but which, in some occasions, may turn out to be **unpredictable**.
There are players who, because of their individual skills, can occasionally gain advantage for their team in particular situations. To a great extent, such situations depend more on good individual tactical skills than on group tactical work.

Level 3

The team presents a **new and unpredictable** tactical activity.
The coach's ability is reflected both in tactically preparing the team and in giving some individual players the opportunity to express their talent.

From the above considerations, we can conclude that when two teams play a match, they demonstrate both their players' technical-tactical level as well as the degree of effectiveness of the coach's coaching method.
If, for coaching purposes, we imagine a match between teams with different skills, we can theorize which of the two has the greater chance of success. This is the common practice that enables coaches to analyze their team's matches with a critical mind, acknowledging, even if in very general terms, their team's tactical ability level.

Virtual matches

The following six possible virtual matches can be used by a coach both to assess his own team's behavior during a match and to understand how effective his tactical coaching is.

- If the team has a **"level 1"** tactical knowledge, and the opposing team is at the same level, the chance of success or failure is the same for both teams. Predominance depends only on occasional individual initiative.

- If the team has a **"level 1"** tactical knowledge, and the opposing team is **"level 2"**, the risk of failure is greater. In fact, the players of the level 1 team are not in a position to take the opponents by surprise, and therefore the opponents manage to intercept many passes; or, the players of the level 1 team play with ineffective ball possession and cannot build up offensive action after   stealing the ball. Nevertheless, the level 1 team may still have a certain margin of success, since even though it is true that the level 2 team has some players who can make unpredictable moves, it is generally characterized by a simple tactical organization which can easily be countered by carrying out effective countermoves.

- If the team has a **"level 1"** tactical knowledge, and the opposing team is **"level 3"**, the latter has a tremendous advantage as its players have highly developed technical-tactical qualities.

- If both teams are **"level 2"**, the chance of success depends on how surprising and unpredictable the schemes applied turn out to be.

- If the team has a **"level 2"** tactical knowledge, and the opposing team is **"level 3"**, the latter has an obvious advantage; in fact, the high tactical ability of its players enables them to apply various and unpredictable forms of cooperation.

- If both teams are **"level 3"**, the chance of success depends on the individual players' ability to apply their skills in the favorable occasions that may occur during the match.

Conclusion

It is obvious that level 1 tactical knowledge is insufficient, level 2 is slightly more sufficient, and that level 3 must be a coach's maximum professional goal.

While it is normal for children from ages 10 to 13 to show tactical deficiencies, since experience in excelling in team sports increases in proportion to age, the same cannot be said for the players of the competitive youth sector.

In the five years that characterize this age range (13 to 18) and that separate these players from professional soccer players, the exercises proposed by the coaches must enable them to solve complex technical and tactical problems.

The young players must learn to play using a motor activity which is neither stereotypical nor pre-established by the coach; they must practice exercises which provide for technical and tactical situations in response to stimulation from a hostile environment, with an opponent that challenges them either individually or as an organized group that tries to put them in difficulty.

Coaching one's team with the objective of imposing "one's own play" is a big mistake, since the presence of opponents strongly influences the behavior of all the players. At the end of the match, the coaches that make this mistake often find themselves disappointed by the behavior of their players, whose only fault was that they were unable to practically apply their coach's utopian tactics.

The correct mental attitude is to look for ever new and unpredictable schemes, to enable one's team to get the upper hand over the opponents or to influence the opponents' tactical behavior, forcing them to respond with predictable, and therefore easy to counter, tactical movements.

In-depth analysis 8
RELATIONSHIP BETWEEN PHYSICAL LOAD AND SKILLS DEVELOPMENT

"Situational" sports, soccer included, require optimum execution of the technical action even in conditions of high physical load.

High level teams and athletes carry out actions which are faster and faster and more and more frequent, therefore it is extremely important that these players have the ability to react to the rapid and dynamic change of the situations in conditions of intense body and muscle involvement.

As a consequence, complex forms of coaching are used more and more. An example would be the use of simulations of competitive situations, allowing a coach to coach the mental processes of performance (receiving and processing information) and the physical requirements at the same time.

We can assume that some matches are lost because of deterioration both in the physical-athletic conditions and in the important psycho-cognitive requirements connected with performance (for example, gathering and processing information, ability to react, ability to stay focused, emotion control, determination in achieving success, etc.).

In order to achieve positive results, it is important to organize practice exercises in which the athlete must both receive and process information from the surrounding environment, as well as withstand considerable physical intensity.

We think that technical and tactical coaching must be organized with a physical load characterized either by a match-like physical involvement, or even by a greater intensity, provided the correct motor movement can be maintained.

Numerous studies have shown that, with respect to the ability to react to environmental stimuli, poor performance occurs when the warm-up is not carried out, while very good performance occurs where there is a high physical load. For this reason, we recommend that, before a match or at the beginning of the practice session, the warm-up should apply a body and muscle load similar to that required in a match.

In addition, if the objective is to effectively improve will power, motivation, emotion control, etc., in certain circumstances the practice sessions should apply conditions of maximum physical load, even if this means an increase in technical mistakes.

Also Available from Reedswain

Finally, we would like to repeat our belief that, since optimum functioning of muscle and body abilities during a match is guided by the player's technical competence, physical abilities and specific technical abilities must absolutely be coached at the same time.